TRACING YOUR LONDON ANCESTORS

FAMILY HISTORY FROM PEN & SWORD

Tracing Your Yorkshire Ancestors
Rachel Bellerby

Tracing Your Royal Marine Ancestors
Richad Brooks and Matthew Little

Tracing Your Pauper Ancestors
Robert Burlison

Tracing Your Labour Movement Ancestors
Mark Crail

Tracing Your Army Ancestors
Simon Fowler

A Guide to Military History on the Internet
Simon Fowler

Tracing Your Northern Ancestors
Keith Gregson

Your Irish Ancestors
Ian Maxwell

Tracing Your Scottish Ancestors
Ian Maxwell

Tracing Your Air Force Ancestors
Phil Tomaselli

Tracing Your Secret Service Ancestors
Phil Tomaselli

Tracing Your Criminal Ancestors
Stephen Wade

Tracing Your Police Ancestors
Stephen Wade

Tracing Your Jewish Ancestors
Rosemary Wenzerul

Fishing and Fishermen
Martin Wilcox

TRACING YOUR LONDON ANCESTORS

A Guide for Family Historians

Jonathan Oates

Pen & Sword
FAMILY HISTORY

First published in Great Britain in 2011 by
PEN & SWORD FAMILY HISTORY
an imprint of
Pen & Sword Books Ltd
47 Church Street
Barnsley
South Yorkshire
S70 2AS

Copyright © Jonathan Oates 2011

ISBN 978 1 84884 130 7

Typeset in Palatino and Optima by
CHIC MEDIA LTD

Printed and bound in England by
CPI UK

Pen & Sword Books Ltd incorporates the imprints of
Pen & Sword Aviation, Pen & Sword Maritime, Pen & Sword Military,
Wharncliffe Local History, Pen & Sword Select, Pen & Sword
Military Classics, Leo Cooper, Remember When,
Seaforth Publishing and Frontline Publishing

For a complete list of Pen & Sword titles please contact
PEN & SWORD BOOKS LTD
47 Church Street, Barnsley, South Yorkshire, S70 2AS, England
E-mail: enquiries@pen-and-sword.co.uk
Website: www.pen-and-sword.co.uk

CONTENTS

ACKNOWLEDGEMENTS

I have been greatly assisted by a number of kind friends who also happen to be knowledgeable upon subjects which I am not. This roll of honour includes Ruth Costello, John Coulter, John Gauss, and Professor Brian Kemp. Any errors, of course, are mine alone.

The book is dedicated to the memory of my late father-in-law, William Howard Bignell (1927–2009), who was born in Middlesex and whose ancestors lived in London since at least the early nineteenth century.

William Howard Bignell outside Woollaston Road, London, 1959.
Mrs Bignell's collection

INTRODUCTION

Many people have lived, and do live, in London; perhaps about one fifth of the population. Some have been born there, some have moved there and some have died there. Some spent part of their lives here; some spent it all there. Some became famous and important figures in history, though most did not. All, however, made their imprint on the records created at the time, though some more than others. Their descendants may still live in London, but many may live elsewhere, either in other parts of the country or overseas. This book is a guide to finding out more about your London ancestors.

But this is easier said than done. When it is found that an ancestor has been born in or moved to London, it is not quite the same as discovering that they were from a small village. London and its myriad records, especially to those who do not now live there, can seem like a large and difficult mass to digest. It does not have to be so. This book will indicate the sources and where to find them, what they contain and how useful they are.

It is now certainly an opportune moment to research your London ancestors, given recent technological innovations. The author remembers, in 1997, thinking that the indexing of the 1881 census and its availability on microfiche was a major step forward, but now this seems comparatively trivial. Much of the basic work of making a skeletal family tree; using census returns, parish registers and birth, marriage and death certificates, can be done online, though often with fees to be paid. However, most records which can be used for research are not, and may never be, available electronically and it is these as well as the electronic sources which this book addresses.

Any readers starting to research their family history should certainly begin with both their living relatives and any documents held in the family, such as old certificates, newspaper cuttings, photographs, school reports and so forth. Many books about family history used to state that the 'Family Bible' was a key place to start, but I have never knowingly met anyone who has one of these, so must assume these are mostly mythical. But starting with your older relatives and their family documents is the best, before you visit libraries and archives.

Two abbreviations which will be used throughout this book are LMA (London Metropolitan Archives) and TNA (The National Archives).

The National Archives, 2010. Author's collection

Both of these places are ones which most readers will need to visit several times. Contact details for both are to be found in the Bibliography, but a brief introduction to both will now be given.

The LMA was created by a merger in 1979 between the London County Council Record Office and the Middlesex Record Office, both created between the World Wars. It was located at its present address in 1982 and was then known as the Greater London Record Office, renamed in 1997. In 2005–10, the archives of the Corporation of London Record Office and the Guildhall Manuscripts section were brought to this new site. It holds the archives of the Middlesex Quarter Sessions, the Metropolitan Board of Works, the London and Middlesex County Councils (LCC and MCC), the Greater London Council, parish and Nonconformist archives, school archives (strong for the schools in the former LCC, not for MCC), electoral registers and directories, some Jewish archives, some tax records and records of crime, prisons and trials. It also contains an excellent collection of photographs from the LCC, including many of schools.

TNA was formerly the Public Record Office, located at Chancery Lane in 1838, which slowly transferred to the present site at Kew in the 1990s and was given its new name in 2002. It holds the archives of central government. These include military archives (including First World War soldiers' records), records of the Metropolitan Police, some taxation records, naturalization and some immigration records, a well-stocked library of directories and transcripts of documents and free digital access.

It should also be realized that this book covers what is now termed 'Greater London', but which was before 1965 Middlesex and London, as well as those parts of other counties adjoining London which were in Essex, Surrey and Kent.

Within greater London there are thirty-two London boroughs and each holds historic material and allows access to it. This is done by means of a local history/studies/archives centre (the names vary but they mean the same), which is usually within that council's library service, and is often physically within that borough's central library, or, sometimes, in a historic building. They are staffed by people who have

London Metropolitan Archives, 2010. Author's collection

much experience of local history sources and often have professional qualifications in archive or library work. Some are even family historians. However, these places are often short-staffed and opening hours and services provided vary considerably.

Publicly funded local libraries have existed in greater London since the 1870s as a result of the Public Libraries Act of 1850 being adopted by the council in question and by 1914 few districts except the smallest lacked one. They have collected local history materials, both artefacts and archives, since their inception. At first, these collections were haphazard, but as the twentieth century progressed, they began to be collected and organized in a more professional manner and library services began to employ professionally qualified archivists and local history librarians to oversee and manage these collections. Each local authority archive collects material relevant to the history of that borough, though there may be some overlaps with neighbouring authorities. These places hold the archives of the borough and archives of local people and organizations. They also hold copies of family history sources, such as local newspapers, parish registers and census returns, as well as electoral registers and directories. They will have a collection of local maps for the eighteenth century and beyond, books about local history and a collection of photographs of the borough and its inhabitants in the past. However each place varies in its exact holdings; for example, some may have extensive collections of archives pertaining to civil defence personnel, others may not.

Although most places are happy to give information and advice about research, do not expect them to undertake lengthy research on your behalf – you will have to either visit or pay someone to do this for you. Some archives do have a system where enquirers can pay to have research done on their behalf.

The author has worked in London archives (as assistant Archivist at Lewisham Local Studies Centre and then as Borough Archivist at Ealing Local History Centre since 1999) since 1994 and has researched his in-laws' London ancestors. He has also written extensively on aspects of London's local and criminal history (twelve books to date). He has advised and helped hundreds or thousands of family historians. Hopefully this book will assist even more.

Chapter 1

LONDON

In order to make the best use of the myriad resources for family historians which exist in London, we need to examine what London was and what it became, as well as what it and its inhabitants are now. London, for most people, is the capital of the United Kingdom. For the tourist it is the Tower of London, Buckingham Palace, Trafalgar Square, for the shopper it is Oxford Street and for the sports fan it is the numerous football teams, tennis at Wimbledon and rugby at Twickenham and Richmond. But we need to look beyond these facets of London.

I have lived in London for most of my adult life. When visiting south London in 1988 to see an old school friend, I made the observation that London was not one amorphous mass, not a provincial city writ large, but a collection of villages which expanded over time. Over twenty years on I still think that such a basic description is not a bad one and it is worth keeping in mind.

Roman and Medieval London

There may have been a British settlement by the Thames in what we would now call London, but the city owes its founding to the Romans in the first century. Londinium was the capital city of the province of Britannia. Sacked by Boudicca's rebels in AD 60, it rose from the ashes to become a thriving port and capital city, with a population of perhaps between 45,000 and 50,000 in the third century. Its fortunes waxed and waned over the next ten centuries, and it was not always the capital of the disunited Britain, fought over by Saxon and Viking, but by the eleventh century that role had been reasserted and this time permanently.

It was the City of London, that district of about 675 acres which runs north from the Thames to Aldersgate and west to east from Temple Bar to the gates of the Tower of London, from which London springs. This was well established before the Norman Conquest of 1066. From the twelfth century the City was granted a charter of incorporation and was then governed by a Mayor (Lord Mayor from the fifteenth century), aldermen and councillors from among the city's wards (since 1394 there have been twenty-five). These men made the decisions for the City at regular meetings of courts in session, regulating trade and keeping law and order. St Paul's Cathedral was the centre of the diocese of London, and was also a major landowner in London and in the adjacent counties. The City was also the commercial centre of the nation, giving rise to over 100 livery companies, many of which still exist. Since the seventeenth century it has also been the national centre of finance and credit.

Apart from the City, the financial and commercial centre, there was also the nearby settlement of Westminster, known as a place for royalty, and from the thirteenth century, of Parliament, and centred around the Abbey of Westminster, consecrated in 1065. Many wealthy families owned property there and traders resided nearby to cater to their needs. The Cities of London and Westminster, as they were termed during the Middle Ages, had, in about 1200, a population of perhaps between 20,000 and 25,000, making them by far the largest city in the country; the figure achieved in Roman times was not reached again until the fourteenth century. There were also a number of foreign merchants resident here, including a Jewish community, until their expulsion in 1290.

To the west and north of these two important settlements was the county of Middlesex, first mentioned in a charter of AD 704 and which officially became a county in the tenth century. Middlesex was rural, as was most of England, with scattered manors and was predominantly agricultural in character. It was lightly populated compared to the two urban districts already mentioned. To the east of the City lay the county of Essex, and to the south of the Thames the counties of Surrey and Kent, with Southwark forming an outer bastion of the urban district, just south of the river (a list of current boroughs, with the counties to which they once belonged, appears in the Bibliography). As with Middlesex, much of those counties near London was rural. These places were governed by a patchwork quilt of manors, mostly established before the Norman Conquest of 1066. It will be noted that most of what was then termed London was to the north of the Thames, and it was, as we shall see, to remain ever thus.

Early Modern London

Despite setbacks to the growth of London's population, caused by the Black Death of the fourteenth century, London became more populous.

Tudor London possessed about 100,000 inhabitants and the figure doubled under the Stuarts. Other major setbacks to population were the later plagues of 1563, 1593, 1625 and 1665; the last of which led to, perhaps, 100,000 people dying. Fire in 1666 was far less deadly, but destroyed much of the City, including St Paul's Cathedral. Yet London recovered; people returned after the plague and the City was rebuilt. Confidence in London remained too strong to allow such disasters to overwhelm it. As a Swedish courtier noted, 'the people's courage was so resilient for the English are by nature not easily daunted'. Looking at numbers alone, this is easily demonstrated, with 200,000 inhabitants in 1600, doubling by mid-century and reaching almost 600,000 by 1700.

Growth continued, with Celia Fiennes writing in about 1701, 'London joined with Westminster, which are two great cities but now with building so joined it makes up one vast building with all its suburbs.' It is estimated that in 1750 there were 675,000 Londoners. By the end of the century the number topped the one million mark. This population rise was not organic, for deaths outnumbered births by perhaps 2:1. Rather, it was due to people arriving in London from other parts of the British Isles, and, to a lesser extent, from overseas, often in order to better themselves, sometimes because they were fleeing from persecution. At least 10,000 arrivals came to London each year on average. Cromwell's government had allowed the Jews to return and there were also a number of black people, servants and sailors mostly, from the mid-sixteenth century – there may have been several thousand in the eighteenth century. Irishmen also came to London for work; provoking riots in Shoreditch in 1736 by attempting to undercut local wages. When William of Orange arrived in 1688 and George I in 1714, Dutch and Germans came over in their wake. All this led to a great diversity in churches and chapels in London (and even a synagogue). Many Anglican churches were also built in this period, with churches assigned to populous parishes; in 1730 Deptford had its second Anglican church. After the revolution of 1688, Nonconformist chapels began to be licensed and many sprang up in London.

Many Welsh people have settled in London over the centuries; including Henry Tudor in the fifteenth century and Goronwy Owen, curate and Secretary of the Cymmrodorion Society in the eighteenth. However, the most significant influx was in the 1930s, with the depression leading tens of thousands of people from Glamorganshire and Monmouthshire arriving in west London looking for work. In Middlesex, in 1951, the Welsh were the largest single ethnic group after the English.

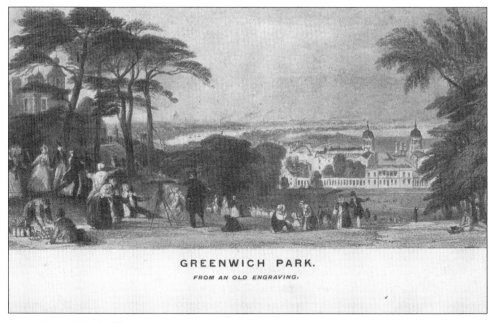

GREENWICH PARK.
FROM AN OLD ENGRAVING.

Greenwich, 1800s. Author's collection

Much of what is now 'Greater London' was rural until the later nineteenth century, as it had been before 1066. Celia Fiennes referred to 'the severrall little towns all by the river, Eriff, Leigh, Woolwich, etc., quite up to London'. Some places were so small that they lacked a public house (Perivale did not have one until the 1920s, and Ealing not until the seventeenth century). Most were tiny villages, but others were quite large and industrial. Deptford and Woolwich became major victualling and shipbuilding centres for the Royal Navy during Henry VIII's reign. The former had a population of about 10,000 people in the eighteenth century, whilst neighbouring Lee had about 300 inhabitants. In Middlesex, Uxbridge and Brentford were large rural centres because of their commercial importance.

There were differences between the urban district and the rural hinterland, then, but there were important links, too. The countryside produced foodstuffs to be sold in the capital, for both people and animals there, and was a ready market for this rural economy. Some wealthy Londoners lived in the surrounding parishes, especially when retired, as attested to by monuments in county churches. In times of danger the two connected in quite a different way: Wat Tyler's rebels of 1381 marched to the City from Kent and Essex and in the seventeenth century royalist clergymen in Middlesex found themselves being replaced by Presbyterian preachers from London. After the Restoration, Nonconformist clergy were forced to live at least five miles from a corporate town, such as London. All this mobility was made possible by the major roads which ran from London through Middlesex and Kent, such as the Uxbridge Road, the Great North Road, the Old Kent Road and Dover Road.

What we would now call local government was, from the sixteenth century, largely in the hands of parish vestries, with the Quarter Sessions court of each county overseeing county-wide matters, such as the administration of justice and dealing with squabbles between the parishes. Quarter Sessions met four times a year in full court, but the Justices of the Peace (JPs) who were the magistrates (chosen from among the ranks of the gentry) could deal with issues in smaller numbers. They also dealt with the majority of criminal cases and many administrative matters, as well as prosecuting Nonconformists and Catholics for not attending Anglican services. The county of Middlesex was made up of 75 parishes and the City of 107 parishes. It is worth noting that Middlesex contained both rural and urban parishes, the latter including, for example, Westminster and Holborn; the former including Acton and Hornsey. Middlesex was 'London' north of the Thames and to the west of the City. Below the level of the county, the parish was the basic unit of 'local government', dealing with transport, the poor and the repair of the church fabric amongst other matters and we will return to it in Chapter 4. As has already been said, in the City, outside the system of county government, the courts of the aldermen and common councillors governed.

London's population and buildings grew in number constantly, if unevenly. There were about a million inhabitants in 1800. Some commentators were shocked at this and William Cobbett referred to London as 'the Great Wen'. Earlier moralists, such as William Hogarth, painted images of terrible desolation in the capital, exemplified by his 'Gin Lane'.

Victorian London

As the nineteenth century progressed, the problems of change were deemed to require different structures to deal with them. Law and order was a major concern, leading to the formation of the Metropolitan Police in 1829, amid a great deal of controversy. Crime was not the only issue. Cholera and typhus wiped out about 25,000 people in a number of

Busy scene in the City of London, c.1900s. Author's collection

periodic outbreaks from 1831 to 1866, known to contemporaries as 'the Great Stink'. Poverty became more apparent to all, especially with the growth of a newspaper- and novel-reading public. There had never been a city the size of London and, whilst it created great wealth, it was also the scene of great deprivation. In 1841, London's population was a staggering 1.9 million, and that of greater London 2.2 million.

Major administrative reforms were felt to be vital to create efficiency and a greater degree of coordination among the many different authorities throughout the capital, many of which dated from the Middle Ages. There was the new Poor Law of 1834, which took away much of the power of the parish for dealing with poverty. It created Poor Law Unions, each a collection of several adjoining parishes. Each union would build a workhouse in order to deal with paupers more efficiently and with a greater degree of uniformity.

In 1855 the Metropolitan Board of Works was formed for what we could term central London. This was not a directly elected body and had little power, but it did at least create a proper drainage system for London: no small achievement. Each parish was given local board status and smaller parishes were grouped together in one board. These local boards principally had authority over public health matters, then seen as an absolute priority, given the outbreaks of epidemics. For those districts outside London, such new legislation was not compulsory. But some parishes did elect to become local boards and so removed power in secular matters from the parish to the local board, where members were elected. Ealing became a local board in 1863 and Acton in 1866. Local boards levied rates to pay for their activities, but they remained limited in their powers and had small numbers of staff; officials were often appointed on a part-time basis and were free to undertake private contracts.

Another major change was the transport revolution of the nineteenth century. Until the 1830s, transport was predominantly horse-powered. Stage coaches ran regularly in both directions along the great thoroughfares to and from the centre of London. The canal network from the late eighteenth century was an important conduit for manufactured goods to London and beyond, as was the Thames from Roman times. But for most people, movement was by the speed of their feet. The coming of the railways changed all that. London's first commuter railway line was the London and Greenwich Railway in 1836, to the west there was the Great Western Railway from 1838 and Richmond had a railway station from 1849. More soon followed. These did not instantly transform what were hitherto villages into bustling suburbs, but did lay the long-term foundations for binding the former to the centre more tightly. This was accelerated in subsequent decades, with improved services, and also the building of the Underground. The first stretch was opened in 1863 and over the next decades many more lines were built. This made commuting far more attractive an option.

Trains did not kill off the stage coach instantly but they helped hasten its demise. By the late nineteenth century, the roads were still full of horse-drawn vehicles, though those for passengers were for relatively short distances only. Motor cars first appeared in the 1890s, but strict speed limits were set for them by the new county councils (10 mph being Middlesex's limit). By the turn of the century, the internal combustion engine was making further gains, replacing the horse buses and horse trams with electric trams and motor buses. These allowed, at last, the working man to live further from his place of work than was hitherto possible, because fares were relatively low compared to alternative forms of transport.

In the mean time, the areas of Middlesex, Surrey, Kent and Essex which were nearest to the capital began to witness startling changes. For example, there were 108,953 people in West Ham in 1881, but 204,893 in

London Bridge, c.1900s. Author's collection

1891. Other places witnessed less sudden growth, but many former villages were becoming more akin to towns, with numerous social amenities, clubs, a diversity in religion never seen before, as well as larger populations, brought about partly by a greater disparity between death and birth rates, but also because more people were moving there; some from central London. The gap between the populations of 'rural' outer London and urban inner London was beginning to narrow, with a total of 5.5 million in 1891 of whom 4.2 million lived in the centre.

A major administrative change came as a result of the Local Government Act of 1888. This created the London County Council (LCC), the capital's first elected representative body, which replaced the Metropolitan Board of Works. It had wide powers over the new county of London, which was 74,816 acres or 117 square miles. These powers increased as time went by, so by the mid-twentieth century it had control of transport, housing, education, sewerage, parks and the fire services amongst others and was a political prize which was strongly contested. In 1934, Herbert Morrison captured the county for Labour. In 1922 its headquarters was the purpose-built County Hall on the Thames. Below the level of this were, from 1900, twenty-eight metropolitan boroughs (ten were north of the Thames, the remainder to the south). These were parishes and local boards which had been in the counties of Middlesex, Kent, Essex and Surrey. Most of these new boroughs were made up of two or more neighbouring parishes. The boroughs were vastly different in terms of both acreage and population; in the 1920s, for instance, Holborn had an acreage of 405 and a population of 43,192, whereas Wandsworth had 9,107 acres and 328,307 inhabitants. These new boroughs superseded the administrative powers formerly held by the parishes and Quarter Sessions.

Middlesex County Council was another creation of the 1888 Act and it headed a much reduced county of Middlesex, with those districts nearest the centre, such as Hammersmith and Holborn, being incorporated into the LCC. Middlesex was now one of the smallest counties in England but had similar powers to the LCC. In the early twentieth century, Middlesex comprised borough councils and urban and rural district councils (formed by legislation of 1894) and some of the latter merged with the former as time went by. Twickenham incorporated Teddington in 1937, just as Ealing had been amalgamated with Hanwell, Greenford and Northolt in the previous decade. In 1939 there were twenty-six local authorities, of varying sizes in population and acreage. The City was, as always, unaffected by these changes and the square mile continued to be governed by its medieval institutions and to have a separate police force. By 1911, there were about 7 million people resident in greater London. It was a great metropolis indeed.

Modern London

As the twentieth century progressed, there was more and more housing in and around London to meet the needs of an increased population. Because of transport innovations, it was now even more convenient to work in central London but live in the suburbs and Middlesex – John Betjeman's 'Metroland' – was created, though this entailed the destruction of the rural and agricultural county that Middlesex had been until the late nineteenth century. People moved out of central London and to housing estates in what had been the countryside. Some were built privately, some by public expenditure, by the LCC, including the Cuckoo estate in Hanwell, Middlesex, and the Bellingham and Downham estates in Lewisham. By the 1930s, London had a population of 8 million, but by now only half lived in central London. After the Second World War, the pace of moving from the centre sped up, with people moving to new towns in the south of England, away from the bombed estates of central London. Despite mass immigration and high rise flats after 1945, the population of London declined to about 7 million.

More administrative change occurred in 1965. The Government of London Act of 1963 resulted in the abolition of the historic county of Middlesex, leaving only the name as part of postal addresses and as the name of a cricket team. The LCC was also no more. What resulted was a name for a new urban sprawl: Greater London. It had a new council, the Greater London Council (GLC), elected to oversee strategic roles, namely in planning, transport and the environment. There was also an Inner London Education Authority which was responsible for education in the former LCC area. The old borough councils were abolished as districts and were amalgamated with their neighbours; often two or three authorities becoming new London boroughs, with either new names or the name of the largest former unit. They had increased powers compared to the old boroughs. In all there were now thirty-two boroughs (far less than hitherto), some of which had been in counties previously outside both Middlesex and London, such as Barnet (Hertfordshire), Bromley, Bexley and Beckenham (Kent) and Kingston, Richmond and Croydon (Surrey). Some parts of Middlesex were transferred to Hertfordshire and Surrey. Of these new boroughs, twelve were south of the river and twenty were to its north.

The GLC did not last long. After only twenty-one years, it came to an end, the loser in the battle between its socialist leader and a Conservative government. Its powers were given to either the London boroughs or to central government. At the beginning of the twenty-first century, however, the Greater London Authority was created, headed at first by the last leader of the GLC. It had less powers than the GLC, but shared the same strategic function for London's government. It also gave its mayor the responsibility for the Metropolitan Police, a function previously of the Home Secretary. None of these changes affected the City of London, which was now the only remaining medieval corporation in England.

Local government has changed much over the centuries. So has the face of London, and not only the built environment and transport networks. The population, both in numbers and composition, has altered considerably, too. But it is not the case that the population of London in 1800 for example, was a homogeneous one, in terms of race or religion. Of the million inhabitants, there were Irish Catholics, descendants of French Huguenots, Jews and black people, as well as a majority of English Protestants. Since then, people from across the globe have settled in Britain; many of them in London. In the nineteenth century most had come from Europe, but after 1945 many came from the Commonwealth, too. London has always been a city of great contrasts: between the very rich and the very poor. Celia Fiennes wrote of the 'Citty of Westminster' that there were 'many of these Noblemens houses built into very fine squares' and there were also the royal palaces. Then there was Gin Lane and the riots of the eighteenth century. Despite reforming legislation and other social advances, similar inequalities exist now.

The London of the twenty-first century is not something to be described quickly nor simply; much the same could be said of the London of previous centuries, too. There are many excellent books which survey London's history (some are listed in the Bibliography). We shall now begin to examine the sources for information about the denizens of London.

Chapter 2

LISTS OF LONDONERS

There are many lists of Londoners, but there is no one list; nor could there ever be; London is too large and its population is ever changing, as has been noted in the previous chapter. Perhaps the nearest approximation are the census returns. These are indeed the best known and the most accessible family history source and they give the fullest information on individuals. But there are others, such as directories and electoral registers. This chapter will take each in turn, assessing their research value, their limitations and any pitfalls which may entrap the unwary.

The Census

A census is, at its most basic, a list of people in one particular district at a given time. The first censuses were in Roman times, but for our purposes, they are of rather more recent date. Irregular censuses have been taken in London since the late sixteenth century; there was a census of the parish of Ealing in 1599, listing, by household, all 428 individuals, with occupations and ages of each (accessible at TNA or as a published work at Ealing Library). However, this is very much the exception. A century later, a number of City parishes undertook censuses of all householders only, and these survive at the LMA. Then there is one for Harefield for 1699 at TNA and a couple of other City parish censuses for 1733 (held at LMA).

The first census to cover Britain as a whole was in 1801 and they have been held every ten years thereafter except for 1941, though it is usually stated that they are of no use to the family historian until 1841 when the census returns had to include the names of each inhabitant. Yet, again, there are exceptions; for a minority of London parishes, including Pinner, Hendon, Hackney, Ealing and several of the city parishes, there are lists of names for some in the pre-1841 censuses; in Ealing's case for 1801 and 1811 and for Hackney's for 1811, 1821 and 1831. A few also exist for Surrey; mostly located at Surrey History Centre, or, for Croydon, at Croydon Archives. Full listings can be found in Jeremy

Gibson and Mervyn Medlycott, *Local Census Listings, 1522–1930*. These pre-1841 censuses, are, however, only lists of names of householders, with numbers for each household, divided by sex and with numbers of adults engaged in agriculture, trade or 'other'. Yet they are worth investigating. These are usually found in the parish archives, for it was the churchwardens and overseers who undertook these surveys. None feature on ancestry.co.uk, so a visit to the local authority archive in question is necessary.

More comprehensive than these are the better known census returns for 1841. They are arranged by registration district, each of which encompassed a number of parishes, then by parish and then by household, so it is immediately clear who was part of that household – perhaps just one individual; for institutions such as boarding schools, prisons or workhouses, numbers are in double or triple figures. For each household, the names of each individual are listed, one line for each and usually in order of seniority (husband, then wife, then children, then servants, if any, then visitors, if any), but then the details are vague. For children up to the age of 15 years, the age at last birthday is given; but those older than 15 usually have their ages rounded down to the nearest multiple of five years. So a 22 year old would be listed as 20; a 59 year old as being 55. Occupations, too, are given. For children under 5 and most wives there is usually a blank. Places of birth only tell whether the individual was born in the same county or not to the one they were living in. Addresses can also be vague. For those living in central London, a street name is usual (but rarely a number); but for those living outside central London, the street name might be given, though house names are usually listed for larger houses, and for public houses. Sometimes only the name of the parish is given, with no indication as to location therein. This is because these houses had no more precise address. Please note that the number in the column to the far left of each census page is not a house number but for administrative purposes only. This seems to cause much confusion among some researchers.

The census for 1851 is an improvement on the previous one, and its format is duplicated in the remaining census returns for the rest of the century. As well as name, address and occupation, the age at last birthday is given; for infants under one, their age in months is stated. Relationship to head of household is given, and the head of the household is usually the husband. Exact birthplace is there; usually this means the parish and county of birth, but this could be merely the city of birth, e.g. London, Birmingham, or if overseas could be merely the country of birth, for example, Ireland. Unfortunately those whose names appear on the return did not always know where they were born; they might put the nearest large town or the village where they recalled spending their childhood and in both cases neither might be where they were actually born. Finally there is a column for 'Disabilities'. This is rarely completed, but sometimes physical or mental disabilities are noted. The censuses for 1861–91 are arranged likewise.

There are a few minor alterations in the 1901 census; there is a column denoting whether the individual is an employer of labour or an employee. The wording on the column for disabilities is less harsh (the term 'idiot' is dropped). Greater changes are evident in the 1911 census. Each household is now given an entire page to itself. It also notes how many children, not always accurately, had been born to the married woman listed and how many are still alive (whether or not residing with the main family unit). It also states for how long the woman has been married. The signature of the householder is also noted at the bottom of each page; he or she was asked to sign it to verify the accuracy of the return.

As said, a census has been taken each tenth year in Britain since 1801 save for 1941 (those for 1931 were destroyed in the Second World War). They are, however, closed for 100 years; thus at time of writing those for 1921 onwards are not available for consultation. This is because those completing them were given a guarantee of privacy in the Census Act of 1920 in order to make the information given as accurate as possible; the census of 1911 was opened in 2009, albeit with the columns for 'relationship to the head of the household' and 'Disabilities' blanked out until complete revelation in January 2012. This was because the guarantee of secrecy was not made until after 1911.

Census returns are a very valuable source of information for family historians, perhaps the most important single one. They give a mass of very useful information which is not only of worth in itself, but as with much that is learnt in the course of family history, it provides further clues for the next steps in your journey. For example, knowing the age and place of birth provides clues for finding a copy of the relevant birth certificate and/or baptism register. And this information can lead to the discovery of the parents of the named individual. It should also give a rough idea of when the marriage took place (if indeed one ever did).

And they are easily accessible. Once it was a matter of visiting the particular local authority archive for the district in question or the Public Record Office (now titled TNA) and winding through microfilms of usually unindexed census returns (researchers being likened to 'things possessed' or 'winding like demons' to quote a former colleague of the author). Now it is easy. The census returns for 1841–1901 have been digitalized and are available online from the ancestry.co.uk website. This can be viewed on any computer in return for a subscription fee, or for free at many public libraries in the UK. Searches can be made on each census by name and then by age and county. This should produce the census page on which the sought-for name is to be found.

The 1911 census, at time of writing, is not available on ancestry.co.uk, but can be searched for free online at Findmypast. The free online version is only an index, but one which gives name, age and place of residence (registration district and county). To see further details, such as occupation, birthplace and address, as well as the rest of the household, a fee must be paid, which can allow the viewer to see the copy of the original return or a transcript. The former costs more but is worthwhile because the quality of the transcription is not high. On looking at the transcription for my grandfather-in-law, I was surprised to learn he worked at Bickfords. The actual return showed that his place of employment was Pickford's. Or TNA can be visited and the entire page can be viewed free of charge. If the researcher lives in London this might be the best option, because there is so much else that can be seen there, as we shall note throughout this book.

Although the census is a very valuable and indispensable tool, it does have its shortcomings. Ages, for instance, are often suspect (and not just for age-conscious women). For instance, the 1871 census lists Thomas Smethurst, a Kensington householder, as aged 60. Using this evidence alone, one would deduce that he was born in either 1810 or 1811. Yet his death certificate, issued in 1873, gives his age as 68 and on his apprenticeship certificate, his birth is noted as being in 1804. It would seem, in the face of the other evidence, that the age on the census is incorrect, therefore. Birthplaces can sometimes apparently alter over time, too, perhaps because the exact birthplace was uncertain. Occupations, too, can be deliberately falsified; although there were thousands of women in nineteenth-century London who walked the streets to earn money, they are usually listed as being servants, milliners or laundry workers. Yet for all these issues, the census is a critical resource for the family historian, though it was taken only every ten years and much can change between these milestones.

There are other lists of Londoners, too, which are a little less known, but are of great use.

Directories

It is normally stated that these books were first published in London in 1677 (which lists merchants only), but there is a London directory at Lambeth Archives for 1638. Generally, they list householders and business owners, with addresses, and were published regularly in the following centuries, even though the next London directory after 1677, was Kent's in 1736. From then on, there were a number of other published directories. County directories covering Middlesex (as well as the other counties around London) were produced by Pigots from 1822 to 1840. By the 1840s, Kelly's were producing these directories, and they ceased to be multi-county, but covered either London or Middlesex or other counties. They are subdivided by parish, though smaller parishes are often lumped together; such as Greenford, Northolt and Harrow. They give a brief account of the parish/es and then a list of 'Clergy and Gentry' (later termed 'Court Directory') and then 'Professions and businesses'. Addresses are not usually given for those parishes outside central London, though house names for the gentry are usually given. There are also separate listings of London businesses in alphabetical order and by trade/profession. By the early twentieth century, these county directories often list telephone numbers, too. The numbers of people listed are very small, but if one's ancestors are amongst them, these county directories are a useful source. For those outside these charmed circles, the directories are frustrating.

A number of 'Court Directories' for London were issued from the late eighteenth century until the 1920s. These included *Boyle's Court Guide* and *The Royal Blue Book*. These listed affluent Londoners, in alphabetical order, giving their addresses, and were published at regular intervals.

By the later nineteenth century, Kelly's local directories were being published for most districts of London, each covering several parishes. They were produced each year, so were far more regular in appearance than the census returns. They were also far more socially comprehensive, listing all householders in alphabetical order, not merely the affluent. They were usually produced in the autumn before the year which is stated on the spine. So the Kelly's directory for Brentford, Acton, Ealing and Chiswick for 1887/1888 would have been compiled from information obtained in the autumn of 1886. They were subdivided into a number of sections. The first covered public office-holders, churches, schools and charitable and societies, and other general information about the locality. But the next three sections are probably of most importance to family historians.

Kelly's directory for Middlesex, 1933. Mrs Bignell's collection

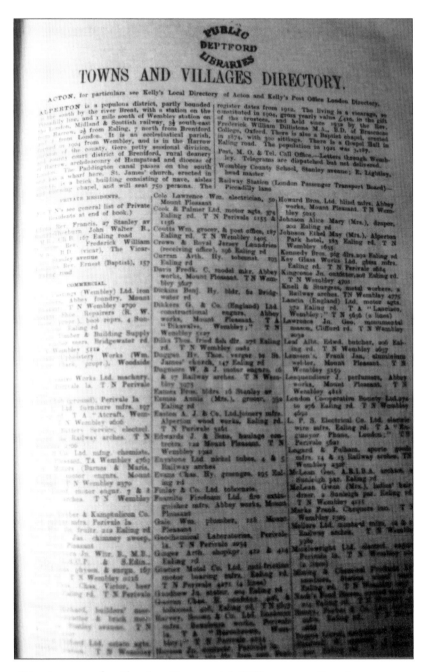

Directory page for Alperton: Commercial, 1933. Mrs Bignell's collection

The first of these is a list of streets in alphabetical order. Under each is a list of householders or businesses which were located in that street, with house numbers and names if applicable. The latter were far more common then than now, and streets were often subdivided into smaller units. The second is a list of householders in alphabetical order, though for the minority of female householders, only Miss or Mrs is given. Finally, there is a list of business proprietors, again in alphabetical order, and also a classified list of businesses. However, the only information which is given is the name of the householder/business owner and their address, unlike the census returns. Yet since these books were published each year, they can help trace an ancestor's movements in between the census years. When an ancestor's name disappears, he may have died or may have moved address and other sources may then need to be checked. The list of householders will help determine if he/she merely moved to another address in the same locality.

The information which these books feature can often be very out of date. For instance, the author recalls finding a publican listed in the Acton directories until 1935, though the local newspaper carried an obituary for him in 1930. These errors crept in because either the updating by the publishers was less than rigorous or incorrect information was forthcoming. It should also be noted that, in the case of multiple occupied properties, usually only one named householder is listed in a directory; though there could be perhaps three households living there.

These directories began to fall away in the early twentieth century. Those for Lewisham cease in 1927, those for Sydenham and Forest Hill in 1939. However, although the Kelly's Acton and Ealing directories ceased publication in 1940, Kemp's directories covered Ealing from 1950 to 1975 and Uxbridge until 1977, though they were smaller in size and only gave a list of householders by street; not in alphabetical order of householder. This makes searching so much more time-consuming. Kelly's did continue publishing directories for Bromley after 1945. Although Kelly's ceased to produce Middlesex directories in 1937 (in the same fashion as they had been in the previous century), however, they did continue to publish London directories (which generally covered only the LCC area) until 1991, but these were increasingly for businesses rather than householders. These directories were even published during the Second World War, despite shortages of paper.

The best single collection of directories is to be found at the Guildhall Library, but anyone interested in the directories for a particular district should contact the relevant local authority archive. Most have substantial runs for their district. Some directories have been digitalized and so are available online. A project by Leicester University digitalized hundreds of directories from 1750 to 1912 (www.historicaldirectories. org.uk/hd/), and of these, seventy-four were for London. Yet this number represents only a small fraction of those which were produced and exist. Ealing Library digitalized all its local directories from 1853 to 1975, but these are only available at the library.

Generally speaking, middle-class districts were better served than poorer ones by these directories. Thus whereas there are Kelly's for Ealing in 1887–1940 and the Kemp's in 1950–75, there are no directories covering working-class Deptford (save for the London directories of businesses). Those for similar districts in east London are better covered, but even there it is limited; for Dalston they are 1894–1908, for Hackney 1887–1915 and for Stoke Newington, 1890–1929. Southall was only covered in the Ealing directories from 1914 to 1935.

However, as the twentieth century progressed, another form of directory was increasingly being produced, and this is often a neglected source for family historians. There is no reason why it should be.

Telephone Directories

Alexander Graham Bell's nineteenth-century invention at first had but a limited impact. Britain's first telephone exchange was located on Queen Victoria Street in London and in 1880 the first telephone directory was issued. There were 250 names in it (mostly from London). However, middle-class householders increasingly paid to have telephones installed at home in the late Victorian and Edwardian periods. In several of his later cases, Sherlock Holmes is noted as having a telephone in his rooms in Baker Street. By 1912, half a million British households had one. In 1909, about 400 households in Ealing had a telephone; though this only constituted about 5 per cent of that largely middle-class suburb.

Numbers of subscribers grew and, after the First World War, most shops, public establishments (such as police stations) and businesses had likewise subscribed, as well as increasing numbers of households, yet still a minority. Since the installation of telephones meant that their owners needed to know the numbers of those people they wished to communicate with, directories listing subscribers began to be published and these survive from 1880. The Post Office ran the telephone service from 1912 to 1981, having taken over the rival National Telegraphic Company. In 1981 the telecommunications and postal services were separated and in 1982, competition began again, with the emergence of Mercury Communications Ltd. In 1984 British Telecommunications (BT) was privatized.

However, the social coverage was still limited until the 1970s, with a majority of middle-class families having a telephone at home by the 1930s. Working-class people only began to have telephones in the 1950s onwards, but by 1990 87 per cent of households had one. However, the near household universality of British Telecom telephones did not last long, for greater competition from other networks, the introduction of the mobile telephone and the increasing inclination for people not to have their numbers listed had, by the 1990s, made these directories less useful for the family historian (perhaps only about 40 per cent of households now subscribe to BT).

Initially telephone directories could be produced which covered the whole of London. From the 1920s, local directories were published. There was a Finchley, Barnet and District telephone directory for 1928, and there was a Hounslow, Heston and Isleworth directory for 1926, but there were none for Ealing and Uxbridge until the 1950s and 1960s. It is also usually the case that the surname and initials (not name) of a householder are given, with address and telephone number.

That said, they are still a potentially valuable source, though less useful for the years before and after the 1970s and 1980s. Arranged alphabetically by name and including the address, it is an easy matter to check whether those sought are to be found. If they are, so much the better, if not, well, the search has probably taken less than a minute. Telephone directories from 1880–1984 can be viewed online at ancestry.co.uk, and the originals can also be viewed at BT Archives, at the Guildhall, London and Bodleian Libraries, as well as at local authority record offices.

Having an address for a family taken from the directories of either variety can be very useful when viewing twentieth-century electoral registers.

Poll Books and Electoral Registers

Lists of voters in bound volumes are not obviously popular reading matter. Yet from my experience, they are the single most sought item in the Local History Centre in which I am employed. Variously known as 'electrical' registers and electoral rolls, they can be a key source for family historians, especially after 1928 as they list all adults resident at any particular address.

Parliaments were first summoned in England in the thirteenth century. From 1429, adult males of 21 and over, and possessed of property worth 40 shillings or more per annum, could vote. They were known as 40 shilling freeholders. However, no lists of these men were ever produced, or if they were, none have survived. Following concerns about electoral fraud, an Act of Parliament of 1696 enabled printers to publish lists of those who voted (not those who were eligible to do so) for any given constituency. These lists are often subdivided by parish, then the voters are listed in alphabetical order. Occasionally their occupation is given. They also state which two of the candidates the voters voted for (most constituencies returning two members), because until the Secret Ballot Act of 1872 such information was open for all to learn.

The key poll books for London are those for Middlesex, Westminster, the City of London, and the counties of Essex, Surrey and Kent. The first known one to survive for Middlesex is dated 1705. Their existence is patchy, because publication was irregular. This was partly because not all seats were contested in each general election, which (in 1715–1911) had to be held at least every seven years. The first known poll book to cover Kent is the one for 1734. By modern standards, numbers of electors were low, because only the propertied could vote. In 1705 there were only about 3,000 electors in Middlesex, though there were about 14,000 in Westminster. Inflation meant that the 40 shilling threshold was being slowly eroded, and this, together with a rising population, meant that by 1790 the electorate of Middlesex now totalled 6,000, though curiously that of Westminster had fallen to 12,000.

A number of Reform Acts in the nineteenth century served to increase the electorate dramatically, making poll books useful to an increased number of family historians. Furthermore, legislation was passed to ensure the annual publication of electoral registers, as poll books were increasingly known. The Reform Acts of 1832 and 1867 resulted in the Middlesex electorate rising from 6,939 to 30,707 in 1880, though population increase also accounts for some of this rise. By 1867 all male property owners whose premises were worth £5 per year and all tenants who paid £12 or more a year could vote. Two years later, female householders could vote in local but not parliamentary elections (contrary to the popular opinion that women could not vote before 1918 – about 13 per cent of women were eligible to vote in this period). Yet although Middlesex as a constituency remained, still returning two members, new constituencies came into being, in both 1832 (Finsbury, Marylebone and Tower Hamlets north of the river; Southwark, Lambeth and Greenwich south of the river) and in 1868 (Chelsea and Hackney).

The third Reform Act of 1884 further increased the number of male voters, by allowing all male householders and all tenants paying £10 a year rent or more the right to vote. The number of Middlesex voters now reached about 68,000, and, of course, this number did not include those in the newly formed constituencies who would have once been listed under the county (e.g. Hackney). The old county constituency was now subdivided into seven divisions, each returning one member. The Ealing division, for instance, included the parishes of Acton and Chiswick as well as that of Ealing. Directories state in which constituency any particular parish was included. Again, new constituencies came into being in London, such as Bethnal Green, Camberwell and Battersea.

There were further reforms in the twentieth century. The 1918 Representation of the People Act stated that all women aged 30 or over or who were graduates could vote in all elections. It also granted universal male suffrage to all men aged 21 or over (abolishing the property qualification), or to those serving in the armed forces who were aged 19 or more. There were also changes to constituencies again; the Ealing constituency consisted of Ealing alone and Acton became a constituency in its own right. It is also worth mentioning the Absent Voters' Lists of 1918 and 1919. These listed members of the armed forces who were serving overseas, given in the constituency in which they normally resided, and providing their military number, rank and unit.

Until 1946 university graduates and businessmen had two votes. The latter had a vote based on residence and on business property (i.e. shop).

Throughout the twentieth century there have been other amendments to London's electoral arrangements. The chief legislation was in 1928 as this equalized the age at which men and women could vote – to 21. This age was lowered to 18 by an Act of 1969. Constituency names and boundaries have changed throughout the century, often reflecting population changes. Another major change occurred in 2002 when two versions of each constituency's electoral register were produced. One was the complete list, as before, which can only be viewed under staff supervision, and an edited version in which electors can choose to have their names omitted (about half choose to do so). Access to the latter is far easier, but is less useful.

Electoral registers are very useful, especially since 1918, because they list, for each year, the adults residing in a household. It is possible to learn when members of the family move away – perhaps on marriage or perhaps they have died. A study of several registers will produce the names of children once they reach 21/18. It is also possible to see who else was living with the family. Especially before

1940, middle-class families would have servants, whilst working-class families might be sharing one particular house. For instance, at 22 Blenheim Crescent, Notting Hill, in 1931 there were three families, including the Pages and the Rushes. However, only the names are given, so all that can be said for any certainty is that those listed are 21 or over, or 18 or over if the register dates from 1970. Far less information than the census, but far more than the directories provide.

Electoral registers are produced every year (except for 1916–17 and 1940–4). The author recalls that on more than one occasion he has been met with surprise and wonderment from researchers when they are informed that none were created in the early 1940s. As the Air Raid Warden in *Dads' Army* constantly stated, 'Don't you know that there's a war on?' Another common misconception is that there is a way of finding where a family moved to when they cease to be listed at a particular address. There isn't, except by looking at other sources, if available. Electoral registers often have restrictions on their being copied, ranging from a blanket ban on anything of any age being copied, to only those of recent years being disallowed. Few are available electronically, though some poll books have been digitalized.

Electoral registers are arranged by polling district and then by address, in alphabetical order. They are not usually listed alphabetically by name, except for a few instances in registers prior to 1918 (eighteenth-century poll books are usually organized in two parts; divided by those who voted for one candidate and then for the other, then by parish, then alphabetically). Some Essex villages have their electors listed in alphabetical order, too. The registers from 1890–1918 hold interesting information about those lodgers eligible to vote (who would not be listed in directories as they were not householders) – as well as name and address, the level of rent is given, as are the number of rooms the lodger had. These can often be just a bedroom, but sometimes more. Often another family member is listed here as the lodger; sometimes this could be the husband of the householder and, in one instance, his rent is noted as 'Services rendered', whatever these might have been! Some poll records, such as those for Westminster (held at the LMA) give, apart from name, address and who was voted for, also the occupation of the elector, too, which is never given in the electoral registers from the later nineteenth century onwards.

They cannot be searched electronically. So unless you have a rough idea of the street where your ancestors lived, they are not the first port of call (searching a register page by page is a lengthy business); you should use another source (directories are perhaps the best option) to locate the address and then return to these registers. However, most do have an index of streets so locating the desired address, when known, is straightforward. It should also be noted that itinerants and transients are often not picked up by electoral registers (or directories for that matter), for someone needs to have been living at an address for a particular period of time or be there when the householder completes the form sent out in October by the council's electoral registration unit. When the author was asked to check whether one of Jack the Stripper's victims was listed at an address where she was last known, he found that she was not listed in the official document, which is not the same as stating that she never lived there. Addresses on civil registration certificates are no guarantee that the individual/s mentioned therein will be listed at the same in the electoral registers (or directories).

It should be noted that voters have to be British citizens, at least until the later twentieth century. Foreign nationals will not therefore be listed. For example, Abraham Feldman, who arrived in London from Polish Russia in the 1900s, and lived in Acton in the 1930s, is not listed at the address he lived in (or indeed anywhere) in the electoral registers for these years. However, he is listed in the directories. Likewise, the author made the mistake that because John O'Shea, from the Irish Republic, was not listed in the electoral register at Cambridge Grove in Hammersmith for 1956, that he had only recently moved there when he was slain by an unknown hand in 27 April 1956. Not necessarily so. Had either man been naturalized, that would have been different.

The best place to see London electoral registers is at the LMA. There is a very substantial collection of them for London and Middlesex for the twentieth century and which are available on microfilm; almost a complete run for each constituency. The British Library, the Guildhall Library and the Institute of Historical Research hold numbers of London poll books and the former has a weighty collection of electoral registers from 1945. Most local authority archives have extensive collections of electoral registers for their particular district, especially for the twentieth and twenty-first centuries. Many of these are on open access on the shelves of the library (apart from the full registers post-2002) and so a researcher can help themselves, though the older poll books may be under lock and key. Some have a few poll books for the eighteenth and nineteenth centuries, too.

However, current constituency boundaries rarely equate with those in the past. Before 1945, some of those parishes which make up the current London Borough of Ealing fell in the constituencies of Harrow (Greenford and Hanwell) and Uxbridge (Southall and Northolt).

Therefore at Ealing Library there is very little electoral coverage for Greenford, Hanwell, Northolt or Southall prior to 1945. Sometimes electoral registers, or some of them, may be held off site or in another department of the council so they cannot all be viewed in one place at one time. It is important, therefore, to know which constituency your ancestors lived in, not just the parish/town. There are no electoral registers for Blackheath, for instance, for this district is divided between the constituencies of Lewisham and Greenwich. Directories will usually note the constituency in which a district falls.

The Middlesex Registry of Deeds

This is an excellent resource if your ancestors were property owners and you know roughly when they were selling property. From 1709 to 1938 there was in existence the Middlesex Deeds Registry, covering the county of Middlesex, which from 1899 excluded property in the newly formed county of London. Only in two of Yorkshire's ridings are there similar registries. The one for Middlesex is held at the LMA and consists of 12,000 index volumes.

In order to use it, you must first check the year in which you believe your ancestor sold property, and there is a long list of names for each year, arranged by letter. Once found, there will be a reference number. Make a note of this and then go to the microfilm which includes that number for that particular year (there will usually be the name of the second party to the deed in the index too). The deeds are registered in that number order. Once the deed has been found, you will be able to read the deed that your ancestor was the principal party to. As with most deeds, it will name the principal parties concerned, i.e. buyer, seller and any intermediaries, with their addresses and often occupations. It will detail the property and the price for which it was sold or rented. There may be a plan of the property attached and there may be conditions attached to the sale or lease.

Other Lists

We have already reviewed the main series of lists of Londoners. But there are many others. From the seventeenth century to the nineteenth there have been fears of invasion and rebellion, especially from the Catholic minority. These scares resulted in governments ordering lists to be drawn up of potential enemies and of those loyal to the Protestant status quo. One of the first of these was the Protestation Lists of 1642.

Churchwardens and constables of each parish had to draw up lists of those adult men who would 'live and die for the true Protestant religion, the liberties and rights of subjects and the privileges of Parliament'. These lists enumerated the parish's Protestant men and the Catholic men; no more information is given. These surviving lists can be found in the House of Lords Record Office; there are some copies at the British Library Manuscripts Room. Two valuable works by the Camden Society (published in 1847 and 1848 respectively) include extensive lists of Londoners; 'The Diary of Henry Maclyn', a very busy undertaker, for 1550–63, which lists those he buried, and 'The Obituary of Richard Smyth', covering 1627–75, with much biographical information about the middling people of the capital. Both are indexed.

Jacobite threats resulted in other lists being drawn up from 1696 to 1745. Following an assassination plot against William III in 1696, lists of London men who took the oath of allegiance to the reigning monarch were drawn up and can be found at TNA (ref. C 214/9). In 1745 those in Middlesex who supported George II and paid for military support appended their names and sums promised to a list (found at the Bodleian Library). There were other lists of Catholics drawn up at other times, known as the Recusant Rolls of 1592–1691, listing those who did not attend Anglican service and so were fined (located at TNA, E 376–7) and during 1778–1857 (TNA again, E 169/79–83). These are national lists, of course, but London Catholics and Nonconformists should be found here.

There was a national Land Valuation undertaken in 1910 and sometimes known as the 1910 Domesday survey. For that year, and that year only, lists of property were made, with owner, occupier and sometimes the amount paid in rates. These surveys have been deposited at local authority archives and are a useful source to find out who owned the premises, if it was rented, unless the occupiers had that privilege. Accompanying maps and books also can be viewed at TNA, series IR.

Most local authority archives have lists of people who have lived in that district. These are always partial; covering only part of that district's current jurisdiction and usually only for a limited number of years. Lewisham Local Studies Centre has a list of Blackheath residents from 1680 to 1940, for instance, created by a Blackheath historian, Neil Rhind. There may also exist indexes to the local newspapers, and since none of these have been yet digitalized, these are also worth checking, though the indexes usually refer to prominent residents, such as politicians, headmasters, clergy and so forth, rather than to dustmen or grave-diggers. The Society of Genealogists' Library also has lists of Londoners on its library shelves.

It is also worth bearing in mind that these libraries often have card indexes to people, places and events which have some connection with the locality. These may well have been created many years ago by librarians and others in the era before IT was used. It is always worth checking these, or asking them to be consulted, because it is a relatively quick task – they are almost always arranged alphabetically and will refer to other sources, such as books or archives, and therefore may be a short cut to relevant information about an ancestor.

We shall come across other lists in this book, but these are usually specific to a particular use, e.g. educational or military, and as such will be discussed under that section.

Taken together, these listings should help establish where families were located in London over the past three centuries; and are of most use in the nineteenth to the mid-twentieth centuries. As ever, they are of greatest use for tracking down people in business and/or with a reasonable degree of affluence, and those who resided in a district for a reasonable period of time.

Chapter 3

CRIMINAL LONDON

B ut I don't have any criminal ancestors, many readers will immediately protest. This chapter does not look only at criminal ancestors, but all those caught up in the process of crime – whether as victims, magistrates and witnesses, as well as those accused of crime. And there were certainly many crimes committed in London. In 1939 there were 94,900 recorded offences and four decades later (with a lower population but more to steal) it was 570,000. Crime was not uncommon then or now. When many people think about London criminals of the past it is of the well-known cases, such as 'Jack the Ripper' of 1888 and the Krays in the 1960s, yet most crime is relatively minor. Only about 0.02 per cent of London crimes in the 1930s were murders. Most were thefts, drunkenness, begging and so forth. If you have criminal ancestors, they will almost always receive more coverage in the press than law-abiding citizens (if they were found out, of course). 'Man kills wife' has great mileage; 'Man has child by wife' does not. John Haigh, an otherwise unexceptional man, killed six people in the 1940s and said that he was, at the time of his trial in 1949, the third most famous person in Britain (Churchill and Princess Margaret being numbers one and two).

The Courts and Crime

There were a number of courts dealing with crime in London. Each county in England was under the authority of two, later three, courts. There was the court of Quarter Sessions, formed in 1361 and lasting until 1971, which dealt with the majority of offences. This met four times each year, but justice could also be dealt out at other times by one or more JPs, depending on the severity of the offence. Thus Greater London was covered by the county sessions; chiefly Middlesex, but also those for Kent, Surrey, Essex and Hertfordshire as well. Then there were the Assize courts, from 1559–1971, which tended to deal with the most serious crimes, although there were no hard and fast boundaries. The Home Counties circuit covered Greater London except for Middlesex; the

Central Criminal Court, also known as the Old Bailey, was the equivalent court for Middlesex. Finally, from the late nineteenth century, there were the numerous magistrates' courts, which dealt with minor offences and passed those accused of more heinous crimes to a higher court.

To take the Quarter Sessions first. Their indictment files and order books give information about the accused, giving name, occupation and parish of abode, the crime they were accused of, details of the victim and the sentence passed.

Fortunately, the Middlesex Quarter Sessions have been published and indexed for the period 1549–1709. These volumes can be consulted at most local authority archives in London and locating a named individual is therefore easily done. Apart from the coverage of these years, searching for those accused of crime is difficult. In this case, original records need to be examined, and these can only be viewed at the county record offices, where they can be seen on microfilm, but unless a rough date is known, searching through each record, or indictment, is a very lengthy process.

An example from the calendar of Middlesex Quarter Sessions for the later sixteenth century is thus:

> 15 September, 25 Elizabeth. – True Bill that, at Westminster on the said day, John Snowden, late of London Yoman stole 'a stone-horse' worth five pounds, five gold ringes worth five pounds, and a saten dublett worth twenty shillings, of the goods and chattels of Edward Dymock esq. Putting himself 'Guilty', John Snowden was sentenced to be hung. G.D.R., 4 Dec, 26 Elizabeth.

It is worth recalling, too, that some activities recorded in these Quarter Sessions, which would not be deemed criminal now, certainly were in the past. One significant portion of these offences was ecclesiastical, though these were dealt with by civil criminal courts (ecclesiastical courts are dealt with in Chapter 4). Before 1689, non-attendance at the Anglican church of the parish in which one normally resided was an offence. Dissenters and Catholics were often fined for not going to church, the offence being partly viewed as akin to treason, for, since 1536, the monarch was also head of the Church of England. This often gave rise to lists of these religious minorities being compiled by the JPs, which, apart from names and dates, give rank/occupation and parish of residence. An Elizabethan example is thus:

> 1 October, 25 Elizabeth. – True Bill, for not going to church, chapel or any other usual place of Common Prayer, from the said day to 1st January then next following, against John Phillips of Hamsted

co. Middx. Gentleman, William Lord Vauxe, George Vauxe gentleman son of the said Lord Vauxe, and William Hollys, yoman, all three of Tottenham; Juliana Burd wife of William Burd of Harlington co. Middx.

Dating of documents of all kinds up until at least the end of the eighteenth century was often given by regnal year, not by the anno domini year. C R Cheney's *Handbook of Dates for Students* is invaluable here. The twenty-fifth year of Elizabeth I's reign began on 17 November 1583 and so the two documents just quoted are dated AD 1584.

Other matters dealt with in the criminal courts include, up to the 1960s, attempted suicide and men engaging in homosexual acts. We should also note that men deserting wives and fathers of illegitimate children may also be found in Quarter Sessions records, thus enabling a researcher to discover the father of a child who is not necessarily listed on the baptism register as such. Sometimes if parishes squabbled over which should pay poor relief to a pauper, the Quarter Sessions would decide this for them.

Although the parish of Westminster is within the old county of Middlesex, it had its own court of Quarter Sessions from 1681 to 1844,

The Old Bailey, c.1910. Author's collection

so any offences committed here should be in the Westminster sessions papers, held at the LMA, but not calendared, as is the case for nearly 200 years of the county sessions.

The Old Bailey court records from 1678–1913 have been transcribed and can be viewed online. They can be searched easily by name, location and offence and the whole transcript of the trial can then be viewed. This is an excellent resource and is worth viewing and making a speculative search for it costs so little time. It is worth noting that the trial transcripts include the names of witnesses, medical personnel, police officers and other law officers, as well as those accused of crime. The transcripts, which vary considerably in size, give the evidence given by all those concerned and the verdict. Until 1907 the accused was not allowed to speak in court in his or her defence – Robert Wood, accused of murdering Elizabeth Dimmock, was the first to do so (he was found not guilty).

Assize records are available at TNA (see ASSI for Kent, Surrey, Hertfordshire and Essex, CRIM for Middlesex), and are arranged by circuit, from the sixteenth century to 1971. Those dated prior to 1733 are,

West London Magistrates' Court, 2010. Author's collection

as with Quarter Session records, usually in Latin, the language of the law until that year. However, it is usually possible to spot the names of the accused and the jurors (the latter are listed separately) fairly easily. These records are not indexed and are bulky, so unless a year in which a trial occurred is known, they are not easy to use. Assize records usually consist of indictments, listing the offences the prisoner is charged with, and the verdict. However, these give minimal information and if depositions survive, of witnesses' evidence, these are much better. Unfortunately their survival is patchy – there are none for Kent prior to 1734 for instance. Some indictments have been transcribed and indexed and can be seen in printed volumes, such as those covering Kent from 1559 to 1659.

Magistrates' court (sometimes incorrectly called police courts) records are another source for the late nineteenth century onwards. They deal with offences which occurred in the district the court was responsible for. The court books are arranged in chronological order and give the date of the hearing, the accused, their occupation, the offence and the verdict. The information is very brief indeed. However, there are no indexes, and given several hearings on each day, searching blind is a fruitless task, but if a rough date is known, a search is worthwhile.

Records of Wandsworth and Wormwood Scrubs prisons are located at LMA. They cover from the nineteenth to the mid-twentieth century and are not indexed but give the prisoner's name, offence, education, occupation, religion, birthplace, and time arrived/discharged.

Police Records

There are also two other major sources of information. The first are the files of the Metropolitan Police. These are held at TNA (series MEPO). They date from 1829, the year the force came into being, and tend to cover the more serious offences, including murder and manslaughter. They contain a great deal of valuable information about the police investigation, though not the trial itself, which will be found somewhere else (ASSI, CRIM, Old Bailey, Quarter Sessions). Principally there will be the report of the detective chief inspector in charge of the case. He had to write a summary of the case for his superiors. Then there may be additional reports, such as that by the police surgeon about the state of the corpse, witness statements, reports by other police officers, transcripts of interviews with the suspect/s, perhaps anonymous letters and press cuttings and police comments on the trial. In the case of unsolved murders, there are usually several letters pointing the finger at someone or confessions which were received by the police years after the crime.

However, their survival is patchy. There are a number of murder cases for which no police file exists; such as the murder of James Wells on Barnes Common in 1894 or that of Karolin Jones in Brondesbury in 1940. Even where files do exist, many are very brief or have been the victim of extensive weeding. The file on the death of Sarah Martin in Hampton in 1861 is very slender, as are those of the Ripper victims of 1888. Thousands of witness statements which were taken in the wake of the murders of Louisa Steele and Vera Page in 1931 no longer exist. On the other hand, information can be copious; there are several boxes of files on the John Christie murders, and that excludes the voluminous evidence taken in the 1965–6 Brabin inquiry into the case.

The other problem is that these files contain a great deal of highly personal information. Murder files, especially those concerning unsolved murders (e.g. the Thames Nudes murders of the 1960s), are rarely available for any crime committed after about 1940. This is because the crime might, in theory, be reinvestigated, and because people mentioned in the file might still be alive. Even files on murders of the 1930s can be given to researchers with pages deliberately withheld, as this author found when investigating the deaths of two women in Soho in 1936. Records of police investigations for the City of London are held at the LMA.

Newspapers

Another source of information about criminal London is, of course, the newspapers, both national and local. As Sherlock Holmes remarked to Watson, 'The press Watson, is a remarkable institution, if one only knows how to use it.' Crime has always been, alongside politics and war, a major staple of newspapers, as a tabloid newspaper saying goes, 'If it bleeds, it leads'. National newspapers will report murders. The eighteenth-century press was often very brief in its reporting of crime and trials, because newspapers had very few pages and were relatively expensive. But in the nineteenth century, they became cheaper and larger, and the local and national press went into considerable detail about crime, especially if there was a trial. The trial of Thomas Smethurst in 1859 for the alleged murder of his bigamous wife was given column after column for a number of issues. The twentieth century saw newspapers having more pages but larger type and more pictures and so less coverage was given to stories. Unusual or

Wandsworth Prison, c.*1980s.* Author's collection

particularly sensational murders, such as those by Neville Heath in 1946 had a few columns, but others were very brief – *The Times* in 1949 and 1950 had, in total, a few small paragraphs about the murder of Geraldine and Beryl Evans and the subsequent trial and execution of Timothy Evans.

Popular contemporary sources may also be worth investigating. *The Newgate Calendar* is a multi-volume work which was once claimed to be as popular as the Bible with nineteenth-century Britons (see www.pascalbonenfant.com/18c/newgatecalendar/). It is a series of lurid accounts of shocking crimes of, mostly, the eighteenth century, many of which occurred in London. They include the story of a mistress who mistreated a servant girl to the extent the latter died, and thieves who shopped fellow criminals for the reward money. The tales are moralistic as well as gruesome, with criminals usually meeting their just deserts at Tyburn. This was located at what is now the junction of Edgware Road and Bayswater Road.

Most crimes are not fatal. These feature regularly in the local press of the nineteenth and twentieth centuries, often under 'Police Court News' or 'Your Neighbour in Court', in which will be listed a number of fairly minor crimes, with accused, nature of offence, victim and verdict. This was a weekly regular feature of the local press. Journalists always used the phrase 'Police Court' rather than the proper name, and it is not certain why, because the court was not administered by the police, but by civil magistrates. A brief account of a selection of criminal cases will be then given, and there will be much more detail than that recorded in the magistrates' court register books. Remember that suicide was a criminal offence until 1961. Suicides are also usually reported in the local press. Or crimes can be allotted a heading all of their own and feature anywhere in the local newspaper, in addition to the 'Police Court News' section, and these usually give a little more information than those appearing under the 'Police Court News' section. One example of the reporting of a minor offence is this one, taken from the *West Middlesex Gazette* of 20 September 1924:

ALLEGED CYCLE THEFT

At the Uxbridge Police Court on Tuesday, before Mr H.A. Button, John Reginald Christie, of Southall, was charged with stealing a cycle from the Hillingdon Boys' School on Set. 11th. Detective Thrussell said that at 6.30 the previous evening he saw the prisoner lying on the grass in Southall Park. Witness asked him his name and he replied 'Wilson'. He told him that he answered the description of a man who was seen loitering in the vicinity of the Hillingdon Boys' school on the afternoon of Sept. 11th, when a bicycle was stolen from the schoolyard. He replied that he was not there, but did sell a bicycle for a friend of his who lived at Uxbridge, but whose address he did not know. When charged he persisted in his statement that he never stole it. Prisoner was remanded until Monday.

A more extensive account of the crimes, together with the verdict, was given in the following issue.

'You can't believe everything you read in the newspapers' is a common maxim and it is always worth recalling, though the same caution can be used about any form of information. Newspaper reports are usually very limited and can be erroneous, too, in matters of fact. The inquest report of a man found drowned in the Thames on 31 December 1888, stated that he had no living relatives except his mother and his brother, but this was not in fact the case. Also beware of newspaper reports made years after a crime. The *Daily Telegraph* of 1953 reported that John Christie had stolen a car from a priest in Uxbridge in 1933, but the contemporary press of 1933 makes it clear that the theft was from his secular employer. This incorrect information has been repeated by writers on the case.

It is also worth stating that newspaper coverage can be distinctively odd. *The Kensington News* in 1949/1950 and 1953 reported the arrest of both Timothy Evans and John Christie, and their initial appearances at the West London Magistrates' Court. But they did not report on their subsequent trials and executions. Late twentieth-century newspapers cover criminal news far more briefly than cases in the nineteenth century, too.

Local newspapers are usually held on microfilm in the appropriate local authority record office. At the moment the British Library Newspaper Library at Colindale holds a great many local and national newspapers, but these are set to move in the near future. Some nineteenth-century London newspapers are available digitally and can be searched by keyword and date, for a subscription fee (http://newspapers.bl.uk/blcs), but can also be viewed freely at TNA, LMA and the British Library. One such newspaper is the tabloid *Illustrated Police News*, which as its name suggests, was well illustrated with line drawings of corpses, criminals, policemen and others; its pictures of the Ripper murders are well known.

Punishment

We should also discuss punishments. Until the Victorian era, incarceration in prison was unusual, except for those awaiting trial or sentence and for debtors (for whom gaol was common up until 1869). Instead, from the sixteenth to the eighteenth centuries, offenders could be whipped in public, as was Titus Oates in 1685. Hanging by the neck was not uncommon, and in the century after the 1720s, it was the punishment for over 200 offences, mostly crimes against property. The theft of goods over a shilling in value could result in the death sentence, but goods were often undervalued. From then on, the number of offences punishable by death dramatically declined so by the end of the nineteenth century only murder and treason remained. Until 1868, hangings were in public – the last man to die in such a fashion was an Irish terrorist – usually at Tyburn in the eighteenth century, though executions for treason usually took place on Tower Hill. From then until the abolition of the death penalty in 1965, hangings took place inside prison walls. Hangings are usually recorded in the press; often in some detail, and there may also be references to attempts being made for a reprieve (often successful in the twentieth century, when only a minority of those sentenced to death were actually hanged) and the inquest on the prisoner.

Apart from such violent retribution, transportation was introduced in the early seventeenth century. This was viewed as a merciful alternative to hanging. Convicts were transported, first to the newly established American colonies, as indentured servants, until the outbreak of rebellion there in 1775. With the discovery of Australia in the next decade, convicts began to be transported there instead, and this practice continued until the end of transportation in the 1860s. Transportation was sometimes for life, but often for a set term of years. Records of convicts transported are plentiful; many have been transcribed and indexed and can be viewed at TNA (series HO; or you can view the originals on microfilm at the same place). The information which can be found is as follows: the name of the ship on which the convict is transported, the date when the ship set sail, the date of arrival and its destination. There may also be details of when a convict won various stages of freedom.

Finally, there are prison records. There are a number of London prisons; Defoe listed twenty-seven (usually termed houses of correction until the nineteenth century) in the 1700s, but the number fell in the nineteenth century and at present there are but eight, most of which date from the nineteenth century. Often the prisoner would be admitted to the gaol nearest his place of residence. Prisoners in south London often were sent to Brixton or Wandsworth; those north of the river to Wormwood Scrubs and Pentonville. However, there is no hard and fast rule about this. There are 'criminal registers' held at TNA (HO 26–7), which, for Middlesex and London are arranged annually from 1791 to 1892 (they can be viewed on ancestry.co.uk). They list prisoners, with date and place of trial, details of verdict and punishment. There is also a physical description, in case the offender escaped, residence, place of birth, marital status, number of children and religion. There is a criminal register index, covering 1805–40, on CD-Rom at www.fhindexes.co.uk Some of these convict records also include photographs of the miscreants. There are also printed calendars of London prisoners for 1855–1949 at TNA, series CRIM 9. Lists of habitual criminals from 1869–76 and from 1881–1940 can be found at TNA (PCOM 2/404 and MEPO 6/1–52 respectively). If your criminal was in Wandsworth prison in 1872 or 1873 you're lucky, for photographs of all prisoners there survive and can be viewed for a fee on line via TNA's website or seen at PCOM 2/291.

Prisoners at work in Wormwood Scrubs, 1900s. Author's collection

Gaol delivery calendars for earlier centuries should be found at the county record offices, listing debtors and those awaiting trial in the period before the mid-nineteenth century. For central London, the LMA has collections for several prisons, including some for debtors. These include lists of those awaiting trial for the following gaols: Newgate (1711–74), Middlesex House of Correction (1755–83, 1823–5), New prison (1725–95), Westminster Gatehouse (1693–1765). There are also calendars of prisoners on whom sentence had been passed but who were still incarcerated – often awaiting discharge, transfer to another gaol or a whipping – these exist for the New Prison (1690–1774), Newgate Gaol (1711–74), Middlesex House of Correction (1710–74), Westminster Gatehouse (1693–1765) and Westminster House of Correction (1732–58). Petitions for clemency can also be located here.

Some twentieth-century prison records are still held at the prisons themselves; you would need to contact them for relevant information, but as with all relatively 'modern' records, data protection may prevent some more recent records from being open to public scrutiny. The author's recent attempts at such contact for the 1920s/1930s did not prove fruitful. The other difficulty is locating the prison where your ancestor was sent. Newspaper reports, for instance, usually only state that a criminal was sent to prison, without stating which one and for how long. Modern critics often scoff at the fact that a life sentence usually only means a few years, but in fact life rarely meant life. In 1884 a woman shot her husband in Hayes, was found guilty, sentenced to death but was reprieved and given life imprisonment. She was no longer in prison in 1901 according to the census.

There are copious records for petitions for mercy and leniency. Petitions can be found in TNA, HO 17 (1819–40) and at HO 18 (1839–54). Formal documents detailing pardons are to be found at TNA, HO 13 (1782–1849), HO 15 (1850–71) and HO 188 (1887–1960). Judges' reports on petitions for 1784–1830 are located at TNA, HO 47, and for the eighteenth century, in TNA, SP 44 Entry Books. Tickets of leave for convicts who behaved well are located for 1853–87 at TNA, PCOM 3–4, 6, and are indexed.

If the prisoner was found to be insane, he/she would, after 1863, be sent to Broadmoor, in Berkshire. Records are held at Berkshire Record Office, though access is restricted. The date of admission/discharge and readmission and death are all easily obtainable by enquiry to Broadmoor.

Non-Criminals

We should also remember the magistrates, jurors and witnesses, all of whom were a crucial part of the judicial process. Magistrates had to be men of some income and social position (from 1744 they had to have an estate of at least £100 p.a.). They did not need to have any legal qualification or experience, though some did, and most were well educated, having attended school and often university. They and the jurors would usually be listed at the beginning of any court records. Witnesses are often identified with occupation and address in trial proceedings.

Finally, we should not forget the victims of crime. Standard biographical information, can, of course, be found in census returns, civil registration records and other sources. However, there was much attention given to murder victims in the press. We know, for instance, far more about the women killed by Jack the Ripper in 1888 than those who walked Whitechapel's streets and did not die such terrible deaths. When Daisy Wallis was stabbed to death at her Holborn office in 1949, the resulting police file went into some detail about her educational, career and romantic history, shedding considerable light on her life, though not, unfortunately, on her killer's identity, which was never discovered. Perceval Key was killed in Surbiton in 1938 and *The Surrey Comet* gave its readers an account of his background, life and interests. However, newspaper reports about victims often give the deceased a glowing character, with friends and family being interviewed and their statements being reported. How true their testimonies are is another question, for people will rarely speak in public against anyone who has died in such a tragic manner. Gravestones can be either terse and to the point, as in the case of Beryl and Geraldine Evans (giving the passerby who has no idea of their fate no clue to what it was), or very poignant, as in the following case, of a tombstone located in Gunnersbury Cemetery which reads thus:

In Loving
Memory of
VERA
BELOVED CHILD OF C. AND I. PAGE
PASSED AWAY
14TH DECEMBER 1931
AGED 10 YEARS
GOD GAVE THE TREASURE FOR A WHILE
TO FILL US WITH HIS LOVE
AND THEN HE TOOK HIS DARLING CHILD
TO DWELL WITH HIM ABOVE

Vera Page was 10 years old when she was sexually assaulted and strangled by person or persons unknown in Notting Hill.

It is also worth mentioning inquests, which, since 1194, have been presided over by a coroner. These courts are held in the case of unnatural deaths in order to determine how someone died (and in the cases of treasure trove). London was divided into a number of districts, based on geography, for the purposes of these courts. Coroner's records, however, are not always easily accessible. First, they are closed for seventy-five years. Secondly, after fifteen years, the documents can be destroyed or weeded. Most do not survive therefore, and in many cases, only a 10 per cent sample survives, partly due to the sheer bulk of records causing difficulties for limited storage. Most London coroners' records which do survive, after the Middle Ages, are held at the LMA.

For a listing, consult *Coroners' Records in England and Wales* by Jeremy Gibson and Colin Rogers. For those which do not survive, see the local press, which for the nineteenth and twentieth centuries almost always reported inquests, though these are always an abridged version compared to the record created at the inquest.

There are many books about crime, especially murders, and the Pen and Sword Books series includes several about London crimes (some written by this author). If one of your ancestors is mentioned in print in one of these it might seem that your work on researching him/her has already been done for you. Think again. Some books contain information which is at odds with the original sources – i.e. the authors made mistakes. As well as being factually inaccurate in places, authors often indulge in theories which may be highly debatable. Read these books by all means, but retain a sceptical mind and consult original sources. Sometimes the best part of these books is not the text but the bibliography! As Miss Marple once told two credulous young people, 'My dears, your trouble was that you trust people. I never have for years.'

It is often easier to find out about the dishonest than it is about the law-abiding, especially if the former were inept or unlucky enough to be caught. The sheer volume of crime has led to a mass of documentation, much of which has survived. Although some material has been indexed, finding criminals and victims is often a matter of luck. The more serious the crime, the more information there is likely to be, but these heinous offences are thankfully relatively very few in number, though they have attracted the most attention.

Chapter 4

ECCLESIASTICAL LONDON

I t is probably hard for most readers to realize how great was the hold of the church over their ancestors, up until at least the early nineteenth century. People not only attended church or chapel, as well as being baptized, married and buried there, but church courts regulated many aspects of morality and also dealt with wills. The established church also had an important part to play in 'local government'. The clergy at all levels were men of great importance. And the Church of England kept records. These archives are of great importance to family historians and because they dealt with the majority of the population, we will explore these first of all in this chapter. The archives of other Christian denominations and non-Christian faiths, will be treated at the end of the chapter.

There were certainly many churches in London; Defoe noted that in the second decade of the eighteenth century there were two cathedrals, 135 parish churches, nine new churches, sixty-nine other Anglican chapels, twenty-eight foreign churches, 'Dissenters meetings of all persuasions; Popish chapels: and one Jews' synagogue'. In the 1920s, it was estimated there were between 1,500 and 1,600 churches and chapels in London.

The Church of England

We shall begin with the Protestant Church of England, as by law established in the sixteenth century, following the Reformation of the mid-sixteenth century (the medieval church is dealt with in Chapter 10). Since the re-establishment of Christianity in England under the Saxons, England was divided into two provinces, Canterbury and York, with the River Trent being the rough dividing line, then into dioceses, each headed by a bishop. Each diocese was divided into parishes, each with a parish church and a rector or vicar.

The diocese of London was founded in 604. It covered most of Middlesex and the City, Essex and Hertfordshire. Parts of Kent and Surrey were in the diocese of Rochester; some were in the diocese of

Winchester. In 1845 there was a major upheaval in diocesan administration, with the diocese of London including some parishes in Kent and Essex which were nearest London, and those City parishes which had formerly been part of the peculiar of the Arches. Later changes included, in 1877, those parishes in Kent and Surrey going back to the diocese of Rochester and, in 1905, the Surrey parishes switching to the new diocese of Southwark.

As well as the Protestant faith replacing the Catholic one under the Tudors, national government played an increasing role in local affairs or, rather, it decreed that local officials, both ecclesiastical and lay, do so. It should be realized that from the sixteenth to the nineteenth century the parish was the lowest unit of both ecclesiastical and civil government, and this has great importance for family historians.

Parish registers and bishops' transcripts

The best known product of this Tudor revolution in local government was the creation of parish registers. In 1538 Thomas Cromwell, Henry VIII's chief minister, decreed that all baptisms, marriages and burials should be recorded by the parish's minister. These were initially recorded on sheets of parchment, but were later recorded in books, and kept safely, with information about all three types of event being recorded in the same book. Most books on family history state that most parish registers do not survive from 1538, but from some decades later, as Cromwell's instructions were either not heeded as zealously as they should have been or the earliest records were destroyed or lost. However, in the case of London, many do exist from 1538 (St Martin's in the Fields parish registers oddly enough begin in 1525). This is probably because these parishes were close to the seats of central government and so obedience was more common than in the more distant parts of the realm.

Initially, only the barest of details were recorded – names of the parties involved (for baptism, the names of the child and parents, for marriages both parties and for burials the name of the deceased) and the date of the event. During the Civil Wars and Interregnum of the 1640s and 1650s, however, record keeping was neglected and often entries in parish registers went unrecorded. This was because many Anglican clergy were ejected from their benefice, because of their loyalty to the King and were replaced by Presbyterian ministers, who did not use the parish registers. London was a centre of hostility to the King, as were those places adjoining, so for our region, parish registers between 1642 and 1660 (the restoration of the monarchy and the established church)

Wedding picture of William Bignell and Alice Howard, 1922. Mrs Bignell's collection

will be incomplete at best in many cases. The next major piece of legislation was Lord Hardwicke's Marriage Act of 1753, decreeing that banns must be read in the parish/es of both parties on three Sundays before the marriage. Henceforth, marriage registers appeared as separate books to the baptisms and burial registers, and banns were also now recorded.

It was from 1812 that parish registers reached their apogee as regards the amount of information they contain. Parish registers now came in the form of printed volumes which set out the information to be recorded. For baptisms, these were the date, the full names of infant and parents, with father's occupation listed. Marriage registers note the date, full names of both parties, with occupations, and their fathers' names and occupations also noted. There are plenty of local idiosyncrasies; for example, marriage registers for the early nineteenth century parish of Lewisham give places of birth of bride and groom. Names of witnesses, often family friends or relations, are also noted. Burial registers give date, name of deceased, age, occupation and address, which could be only the name of the parish they resided in formerly. In all cases, the man presiding over the service signed the entry to vouch for its authenticity. These parish registers are still in force today, but after 1837, with the introduction of civil marriage, the proportion of the population whose marriages were recorded in parish registers fell, making them less useful for the family historian. Current parish registers are still held at the church in question; most earlier ones have now been deposited at the LMA or appropriate county record office.

That said, a very few originals are held at local authority archives, such as Westminster, Lewisham, Hammersmith and Fulham and at Waltham Forest. However, the originals are almost never produced to researchers. Instead, microfilm copies will be available. Most local authority archives hold some or all of the microfilmed parish registers for their jurisdiction, too. Some parish registers (especially those for 1538–1812) have been transcribed and indexed into book form; some have been transcribed onto CD-Rom.

The registers are arranged chronologically, and vary in the number of entries within them. Fortunately some have been indexed. The best known index is the International Geneaological Index, which is available online. It is possible to search for names within this, which will give the necessary details (but not of burials). However, the IGI does not cover any events after the late nineteenth century, and in any case, is very patchy in its coverage; for some parish registers, several centuries are covered; for others only a few decades, for some, none at all. *The Phillimore Atlas and Index to Parish Registers* lists the IGI's coverage for each parish.

However, the easiest way to search for London parish registers is to use ancestry.co.uk. There are scanned images of London parish registers, baptism, marriage and burial for 1538–1812, marriage and banns 1754–1921, baptisms 1813–1906, and burials 1813–1980. However, these are incomplete at time of writing. Those for the later years can be searched for by name and a digital copy of the parish register entry will appear on screen. The burial indexes are of least use, because after about 1850, most parish churchyards were nearly full and few burials took place there. However, registers continued to list funeral services. One source for burials is the National Burial Index, published by the Federation of Family History Societies, with 18.5 million names of those buried in churchyards and cemeteries in England and Wales after 1538 and is available on CD-Rom and at TNA.

From 1598 until the late nineteenth century, parishes had to return annual transcripts of their registers to the diocese lest the original be lost. Where the original register has been lost, these transcripts are very useful. When looking for the marriage of Thomas Smethurst and Mary

Durham in 1828 at St Mark's Kennington, I found that the LMA did not have the marriage registers for that church from 1825–35. Fortunately the bishops' transcripts did survive, so the marriage could be verified. As with parish registers, bishops' transcripts, which tend to survive to a lesser extent than parish registers, are to be located at the LMA, which is the diocesan record office for London. The county record offices are often also the diocesan record offices; so for those of Rochester diocese, check the Centre for Kentish Studies.

Other parish records

There is much more to parish records than the registers, though these are the best known and most well used, in part because they are the ones which have been transcribed, filmed and digitalized. The other major series of parish records (apart from rate books – see Chapter 5) are those which deal with the Poor Law. A variety of Tudor legislation, culminating in the Elizabethan Poor Law of 1601, created what historians refer to as the Old Poor Law. This basically meant that the parish had to raise funds (rates) and appoint one or more men as overseers of the poor, in order to distribute these monies. The poor were deemed those people who, due to infancy, old age, illness or disability, were unable to find work and thus support themselves financially. Much of this relief was in the way of payments, either in cash or in kind (clothing, shoes, fuel, coal and so forth), and was termed 'outdoor relief'. Yet from 1723 parishes could build houses, or adapt them, in order to house the poor. This was usually accompanied by the need for the inmates to undertake work to offset the cost of their food and shelter.

There are several types of records covering the Old Poor Law. First there are the vestry minutes, which record the decisions taken by the vestry, that body of ratepayers, including the clergyman, who decided how to spend the rates. They met regularly, often monthly. The accounts of their meetings can be wholly non-existent, or might merely list attendees, or they can be very detailed. The vestry minutes books for Hanwell, for instance often record the plight of unmarried mothers, drunken elderly women and children, naming them and what happened to them, often over several meetings. This brings to life the workings of the parish and its methods of dealing with those unfortunate in life.

Overseers' accounts are another obvious source for family historians, because they list the payments made by the overseers and authorized at the annual parish audit. Some account books merely state expenditure as a total, but others itemize it. These may include one-off payments or

St Mark's church, Kennington, 1900s. Author's collection

regular pensions being paid to widows, and if your ancestor was a pauper, this is clearly of interest – also if your ancestor was a member of the vestry or an overseer. The New Poor Law Act of 1834 led to the poor law unions and so the severing of the connection between the parish and the obligatory relief of the poor (for the New Poor Law, see Chapter 7). Parish charities, of course, continued, and references to these and their beneficiaries can be found in charity account books among the parish archives.

Settlement certificates are another source. After 1662, paupers could only claim relief in their parish of birth unless they married and then claimed settlement in their husband's parish. Those lacking settlement rights in a parish were often turned back to their parish of origin if in need of relief. From 1691 the travelling worker could take with him a certificate of settlement from his own parish and on arrival at another parish would hand this to the churchwardens there. This was their guarantee that if he fell on hard times he could be sent back to his parish of settlement. These certificates often can be found in parish archives; the parish of Isleworth had them for 1780–1830, and they now are located at Hounslow Library. From 1692, settlement rights could be earned after working for a year in the said parish, or by owning property.

The best overview of parish archives is W E Tate's *The Parish Chest*. Parish archives are scattered between the LMA and other diocesan record offices, and the local authority archives. This is because the vestry and poor law archives (the records of 'civil government') were often passed to the local authority in the nineteenth century and so often found a home in the local authority archives, whereas the parish registers went straight from the parish to the LMA, but there is no hard and fast rule, with vestry minutes and churchwardens' accounts being found in both places.

Wills

Until January 1858, the church courts administered probate. England was divided between the provinces of York and Canterbury, with the latter having authority for those who had land and goods in the Midlands and south of England. There are 201,133 Middlesex and 86,233 London wills proved by the Prerogative Court of Canterbury (PCC), which, despite its name was located at Doctors' Commons, near to St Paul's Cathedral. Since the PCC wills have been indexed and can be found online at the TNA website (Documents online), it is a simple matter to check here first. Of course, those who made wills, testators, were in the minority – in 1858 it is estimated that only one in ten of the population did so, with more men doing so than women (until 1882 women's property reverted to their husband on marriage), but spinsters and widows made wills. If the will sought is found, it can be viewed for a small fee (or seen for free at TNA). Clearly those with property and money would leave wills, compared to the poor, but one Simon Bales, a cabinet maker who died in a poor house in Westminster in 1840, left a will, too.

However, it is not quite as straightforward as checking this index. Apart from the PCC, there were a number of different ecclesiastical courts in London and Middlesex and it may be necessary to check some or all of these. There was the Consistory Court of London, which had jurisdiction over most of the City parishes; the Archdeaconry of Middlesex Court which had jurisdiction over twenty-six parishes in Middlesex and the Commissary Court of London, with authority over both parts of the City and of Middlesex. The Archdeaconry Court of London had jurisdiction over forty City parishes and three parishes adjoining the City boundaries. Least important was the Court of Hustings, which covered parts of the City but ceased to have any power in 1688. The wills of these courts have been indexed and are available at the LMA. Calendars of wills are also available at the Society of Geneaologists' Library; and online at British Origins.

Lambeth Palace Library has the wills from the deanery of the Arches, a peculiar of the Archbishop of Canterbury, and so outside the jurisdiction of the bishop's and archdeacon's courts. This had jurisdiction over thirteen City parishes. Another peculiar was the deanery of Croydon, covering wills from various Middlesex parishes, including Hayes and Harrow. Finally, there was the royal peculiar of the Dean and Chapter of Westminster. It had authority over Westminster, Paddington and several London parishes. The records are held at the Westminster City Archives. Gibson's *Guide to Wills and their Whereabouts* lists which parishes fell under which jurisdiction.

We should also remember that those parishes outside London and Middlesex were in the jurisdiction of other diocesan courts – that of Rochester for Kent, so they are at the Centre for Kentish Studies, but those for Surrey are located at the LMA, Lambeth Palace Library, and Hampshire Record Office at Winchester.

After all this, it may come as somewhat of a relief to learn that, from January 1858, wills came under the civil courts. Wills proved from then to date are held at the Registry of the Principal Division of the Family (the address of which is in the Bibliography). There are indexes to the wills, arranged by year and then in alphabetical order. These give the testator, his or her address, date of death, date that the will was proved, total value of the estate (although until the 1880s exact amounts are not given – 'under £50' being stated, for example). The will can then be ordered by filling in a form and paying £5 per copy, to be delivered in an hour or by post. The will indexes up to 1943 are available on microfiche at various places, including TNA, but there are rumours that these indexes will be digitalized, which will be a great boon.

It should be mentioned that wills can give a remarkably divergent amount of information. Some merely state who received the testator's estate as a cash sum. Others may go into great detail about how the estate is to be divided, and who got what. Therefore, a good will should provide names of relatives and how much they were favoured. Wills proved before 1733 will usually be in Latin, the language of the law until that year. Wills proved in the sixteenth and seventeenth century often include inventories, too, and these list furniture in the house, property, animals and any other goods. The executors of the will appointed three or four men to make a list of all the deceased's personal effects, room by room, including the contents of any stables or outhouses. Inventories are usually located with the will. This practice died out in the eighteenth century.

For those who died intestate, there may be an administration, where the court decides who benefits from the deceased's fortune; usually the next of kin. Montague John Druitt died in 1888 without leaving a will and in 1891 it was decided that his brother would inherit his £2,600.

Ecclesiastical courts

One of the most neglected sources for family history must be the ecclesiastical court records. These courts – archdeaconry courts and the bishop's consistory court – were of great importance from the Middle Ages to the mid-nineteenth century. They dealt with heresy, witchcraft, non-attendance at church (these two latter offences were also dealt with at Quarter Sessions, too), assaults on clergy, defamation, perjury, dealing with defaulters on church rates and tithes and brawling in church property, as well as disputes over wills. They also licensed surgeons, midwives, schoolmasters, lecturers and curates.

Unfortunately the writing is difficult to read and, of course, until 1733, written in Latin. They are not indexed. The main class of records are the Act Books, which record the court's decisions and which include a great deal of information about those coming before it and their lives. It is estimated that about 20 per cent of the population would have had dealings with these courts in their lifetimes, so after having exhausted all the obvious sources, these may well repay close attention. Diocesan records are held at the LMA.

Miscellaneous church records

There are many other records created by parishes which may be relevant in your family research. From the late nineteenth century to date, parishes have produced parish magazines, usually on a monthly basis. These contain church news, including references to baptisms, marriages and burials, but also to confirmations. There will be lists of lay church officials, such as churchwardens, Sunday School and youth teachers/leaders, sidesmen and others, perhaps giving addresses. There may be brief obituaries of parishioners who have died, especially giving details of their church membership, service and association with the parish.

Some parishioners left money in their wills to be invested in land or stock and the interest to be used for charitable purposes; sometimes to help feed and clothe the poor, sometimes for educational reasons. It was the vestry who often administered these charities and parish records often include charity accounts and minutes, which could feature as part of the vestry minutes. These often list parishioners who were in the receipt of such monies, which were sometimes paid out annually.

Other records for the twentieth century include electoral rolls, which list all adult parishioners who were confirmed and regularly attend church, and the minutes of the parochial church council, which will list

Coston memorial inscription, Holy Cross, Greenford, 2010.
Author's collection

the members of the PCC, which replaced the parish vestries in 1920.

Physical memorials should not be neglected either. If your ancestor was a prominent figure, perhaps a member of a gentry or merchant family, there may well be a plaque to him inside the church where he was buried. This may refer to other family members and may also list his alleged virtues; telling of his strong religious values, of his charitable nature to the poor, his benevolence to his neighbours and his love for his wife and family. This may all be true, but may not, and your research may well either corroborate the plaque's details or may reveal him as a rotter. War memorials of parishioners killed in the World Wars are often found in churches, as are lists of former incumbents. Some of the older memorials may have been damaged in the Reformation or during the Civil Wars of the following century. It should also be noted that some incumbents are positively hostile to such memorial stones – the author knows one who would be happy if his church was denuded of all of them.

Gravestones in churchyards may also hold interesting information about ancestors. Yet there are a number of issues to note. First, the Burial of the Dead in the Metropolis Act of 1852 stated that churches in central London had to be closed for fear of overcrowding leading to health concerns, and that municipal cemeteries be opened, so the number of burials in churchyards plummeted – this was not true for some churches in more rural parts of London until the later twentieth century. Heston churchyard was still accepting burials until at least the later 1950s. Secondly, most of the families of parishioners being buried in these churchyards were too poor to be able to spend money on gravestones. Finally, the wording on many gravestones has become too worn to read. Luckily, some family history societies have recorded all a church's surviving inscriptions and memorials and lists are often deposited with the local authority record office. Churches built after about 1850 rarely have churchyards.

Cemetery burials became the norm in London from the later nineteenth century onwards. Some were established by local authorities, but there were also private cemeteries, too, such as Kensal Green. Check with the cemeteries department as well as the local record office for cemetery records. Most will search for free if an exact year is given, and will confirm if the burial took place there, and also the cemetery plot, so you can then locate the grave when the cemetery is visited. There is a Deceased online website which may be helpful, and some cemetery indexes are available online; such as that for Richmond.

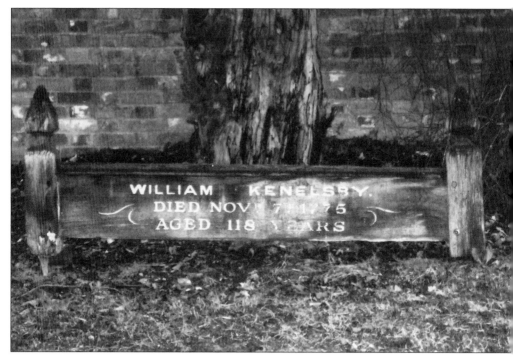

Graveyard memorial, St John's church, Pinner, 2009. Author's collection

Nonconformists and Catholics

Not everyone accepted the ways of the established church of the Reformation. First, there were a number of other Protestant sects who did not adhere to the royal supremacy. These included, from the seventeenth century, Quakers, Congregationalists and Baptists, and, from the later eighteenth century, Methodists. Then there were those who adhered to the old faith of their ancestors. There were Catholics throughout England, with concentrations in Lancashire, Hampshire and London. Catholics were often seen by Protestant magistrates and others as being potentially in league with England's Catholic enemies, such as France and Spain, from the sixteenth to the eighteenth centuries. From 1581, it was an indictable offence to be a practising Catholic and priests could be imprisoned (up to the eighteenth century) and even occasionally (up to 1681) executed. Formal emancipation did not occur until 1829. Having said that, there was also, by the eighteenth century, a great deal of toleration except during periods of national crisis such as the Jacobite rebellion of 1745.

Members of all these groups were strong in London; although as a proportion they formed minorities of the population. They were often suspected of disloyalty towards the state, especially during times of crisis, such as war and rebellion. Because of this, the state took a great, if occasional, interest in their affairs and so records were created about them and their property. Many lists of individuals (mostly adult males) are held at TNA. Pipe Rolls and Recusancy Rolls which exist at TNA (E 372, 376, 377) listing Catholics from 1581 to 1691. Sometimes, parish officials were requested to make returns of Catholics within their parish; several occurred in the early seventeenth century (located in TNA, SP 16/495) one was made in 1708 (TNA, SP 34/26) and others later in the century, and there is a published *Returns of Papists, 1767: Dioceses of England and Wales except Chester* (1989). Another published list is the Cosin's list, *The Names of Roman Catholics, Non Jurors and others who refus'd to take the Oaths* (1862). G L Turner's *Original Records of Early Nonconformity under Persecution and Indulgence* lists many Dissenters, with names and addresses and denominations, taken from numerous sources. The Association Oath of 1696 to William III resulted in lists of London dissenters (C 214/9) and Baptist ministers in London (C 213/170). Quaker lawyers made similar declarations from 1831 to 1842 (E 3 and CP 10). Likewise, there are lists of Catholic lawyers, 1790–1836 at TNA (CP 10, C 217/180/5) and for 1830–75 (E 3). More general oaths of allegiance are located at TNA (E 169/79–83), which cover 1778–1857, giving names and addresses. Quarter Session indictments often list Dissenters and Catholics who did not attend the services at the Anglican parish church and these people were named and fined, especially in the sixteenth and seventeenth century.

Although there was less persecution after 1689, it still occurred periodically, especially for Catholics who were often assumed to be in league with the exiled Catholic Stuart pretenders. This resulted in Catholics coming under the state's attention. For example, in George I's reign, all Catholic property owners had their estates detailed by officials and the reports were sent to the government (records existing at TNA, E 174). Details of Catholic estates for 1625–84 are located at TNA, E 351/414–452.

Nonconformist clergy had to have their premises licensed for worship after 1688. These requests are usually found with the Quarter Sessions at the county record office in question, giving details of the minister and the location of the chapel. Catholic priests had to do likewise, after 1791, and letters by all these men can be found at the

LMA. Close Rolls at TNA give information about deeds referring to use of land and property by Nonconformists (C 54 and, from 1902, J 18). These have been indexed and so are relatively easy to use.

Nonconformist registers of baptisms, marriages and deaths up until 1837 are held at the TNA. Unlike Anglican registers, the baptism registers note the mother's maiden name. They can be searched for online under 'Select More Records and Documents' and then choose 'Non-Conformist registers', and these can be searched for by name. There are a few registers of pre-1837 Catholic churches at the TNA, but most are for the north of England (RG 4) We should remember that Anglican registers often recorded the baptisms, marriages and burials of Nonconformists and Catholics, too, especially for marriages, 1754–1837. Online Nonconformist registers can also be seen at bmdregisters.com and indexes are at Familysearch/IGI.

Finally, we should remember the archives created by the chapels themselves. Some of these have been deposited at local authority record offices, as is the case with those of Anglican churches. For example, Camden Local Studies Library holds records of Lyndhurst Road Congregational Church, Trinity Presbyterian Church, Hampstead, and Whitfields Memorial Church, St Pancras. Apart from registers of baptisms, marriages and burials, these can also include minute books and records of the various organizations which were part of that chapel, such as youth club records or minute books of various committees, both of which include names of participants. More recent records are located at the churches themselves, so application should be made to the minister in the first instance. Most Catholic registers date from 1791, when practising the religion was no longer penalized; most of the registers are still with the churches.

There are also Orthodox churches in London. One is the Russian Orthodox Church, and its archives from 1721 to 1951 are held at the LMA (RG 8/111–304). These include registers of baptisms, marriages and deaths and conversions. Records for the Greek Orthodox Church in London from 1837 to 1865 are also held at the LMA (J 166). Most of these archives are not written in English, but in Russian/Greek respectively, though the catalogue entries are in English.

There were numerous German, French and Dutch Protestant churches in London to cater for the spiritual needs of these immigrants. Most of the surviving registers, which particularly cover the seventeenth and eighteenth centuries, are to be found at TNA, in RG 4.

Non-Christian Religions

From the seventeenth century to the later twentieth, the main non-Christian religion practised in London was Judaism. Following the expulsion of Jews from England in 1290, the Jewish presence was refounded in the 1650s, and grew significantly in the later nineteenth century. Most of the deposited Jewish archives are held at the LMA. These are principally the United Synagogue (ACC/2712) and the papers of the Office of the Chief Rabbi (ACC/2805). The United Synagogue was founded in 1870 and was involved in a multitude of activities; social, philanthropic, educational as well as the strictly religious. These led to the creation of minutes, accounts, deeds, correspondence, photographs and other records. These records can only be inspected by written permission of the Chief Rabbi. However, many of the records of the Spanish and Portuguese Jews Synagogue (one of the oldest synagogues in London), including records of births, marriages and deaths, have been transcribed and published and can be found at the LMA library (ref. 60.58). Records of most synagogues still remain with their creators and so contact should be made with the appropriate synagogue if required. Remember that for boys there should be registers of circumcision, too.

After 1945, with a number of waves of immigration from the Commonwealth, new religions established themselves. These were principally Sikhism, Islam and Hinduism. Relatively few of the archives of these temples and mosques have been deposited with any public record office, so anyone wishing to locate records should contact the individual place of religion.

Remember that most of these records will not be written in English, so having someone with you who is fluent in the relevant language is highly advisable.

Remember too, that newspapers cover the opening of places of religion so may be worth checking if you know the date of a place's foundation. In the nineteenth century at least, local newspapers often listed the principal people at such a momentous event; sometimes souvenir pamphlets were produced which also list those who designed and built the place – often co-religionists.

Religious archives are an important source of information for family history and can hardly be ignored. This is especially the case up until the nineteenth century, when the secular state at local and national level began to supplant their role as regards social care and education. But even afterwards, many people's lives have been affected by organized religion and many have participated in its activities.

Chapter 5

TAXING LONDONERS

B enjamin Franklin once famously observed that there is nothing certain in life except for 'death and taxes'. This is just as well for family historians, and this chapter will concentrate on the latter, which is a less well-known geneaological source than the former. Governments at both local and national level always need sources of revenue in order to pay for their policies, and in the process of their administration, records of tax payers are made and often retained to be used by researchers. Medieval and Tudor taxes, including the well-known poll tax of the fourteenth century and the less well-known subsidies, will be discussed in Chapter 9. This chapter looks at financial levies imposed by national and local government since the seventeenth century. It was in this century that taxation became permanent; hitherto, the monarchs only asked money from their subjects when he/she needed to go to war. How accurate the records are is another question, for it was in the taxpayers' interests to try and reduce their liability by evasion or avoidance. There are a number of different types of tax; those on property, those on wealth, those on income and those on expenditure. The last type (indirect taxes, such as customs and excise) can be disregarded because they are not taxes on individuals, but on spending and therefore leave no records of individuals.

Rates

The longest running of all levies in England, lasting from 1601 to 1990, were the rates. These were first imposed periodically in the later sixteenth century, but as a result of the Elizabethan (Old) Poor Law Act of 1601 usually became a regular annual fixture, though not always – the parish of Lee had so few poor that an annual rate was unnecessary. There could also be additional temporary rates levied on parishes, for example to finance a county prison or asylum. Normally, though, rates were levied in order that the parish could relieve the local poor in cash or in goods. The vestry would set the annual rate at a certain level at so many shillings in the pound and the overseers of the parish would assess the value of each property in the parish. These assessments would then be listed in the rate book, with the figure payable next to the ratepayer's name. Each rate book usually covers several years' assessments, depending on the size of the parish's population, at least until the early nineteenth century. We are thus presented with a list of householders for each year, in a series of books, potentially from the early seventeenth century to the early nineteenth century. Furthermore, it is possible to see how valuable that ancestor's property was compared to others in the parish. There were also separate rates levied for the upkeep of the church fabric, known as the Church Rate, and the Highway Rate, to pay for men to repair roads and bridges in the parish. Every property was assessed, except of those who were too poor to pay and who were in receipt of poor relief (their names are usually featured in books of overseers' disbursement, as noted in Chapter 4). There is usually a note to state whether the rates were paid.

However, there are two caveats. The first is that the survival of a large run of rate books is very rare. For example, those for Hampstead parish only cover the years 1774, 1777, 1779–1826, 1829–55, but those for Holborn exist from 1729 to 1900, with very few gaps. One example of a run beginning in the seventeenth century is those for Ealing from 1673 to 1834, and even then, the first rate book is titled 'volume 37' – the preceding thirty-six having not survived. The sheer bulk and number of rate books for each year for the later nineteenth and twentieth centuries have led many rate books to be destroyed (because of storage restrictions) and so often only rate books for every other year, or every third or fourth year, have survived. During the Second World War, the beaming mayor of Croydon gave an early Victorian rate book to the salvage drive to be pulped for the war effort!

Secondly, the rate books usually do not give any clue to the precise whereabouts of the property, give addresses or name the property, in the parish. That said, some rate books, from the eighteenth century, do sometimes break the parish down into different sections. That for Ealing groups ratepayers as to whether they lived around Haven Green, Little Ealing, Castlebar, Gunnersbury, Ealing Common, Church Ealing and so forth, and using the 1777 parish map we can see where these places were. In the assessments for 1753 and 1754 we see the author Henry Fielding's name and in those for 1808–12 there is the Right Honourable Spencer Perceval, Prime Minister. Those for Deptford after 1730 give full addresses, as do those in the City and Westminster.

In the nineteenth century, the powers of the parish fell into decline and by the end of the century they were taken over by the local boards, the borough or urban councils. These also took over the administration and assessment of the rates. The rate books began to give addresses as well as names of ratepayers and amount of money levied, as well as whether the rates were paid. In 1990 the rates were replaced by the Community Charge, also known as the Poll Tax, which was a tax on adults rather than the property itself. Amidst much controversy it proved short-lived and was replaced by the Council Tax, which was again based on the value of property.

Rate books, where they survive, tend to be found in local authority record offices with the parish archives, and at the county record offices. Few have been transcribed, indexed or digitalized. However it is important to note that these rate books were maintained each year, even during the World Wars, when directories and electoral registers were suspended, so enabling researchers to pinpoint householders during these years in which they otherwise could not be traced.

Hearth Tax

Another useful source for the later seventeenth century are the records of the Hearth Tax. This was a tax imposed on householders from 1662 until 1689. It was payable twice a year in two instalments. Tax payers had to pay one shilling per hearth, i.e. fireplace, in their property. As with the rates, owners with larger properties had to pay more and the poorest were exempt, as were buildings which were for charitable uses. Constables and overseers had to collect the tax, and there is a high survival rate of hearth tax returns for 1662–6 and for 1669–72. The assessments for the other years do not exist because the tax collection was farmed out to private individuals who did not have to send their returns to the Exchequer.

These assessments are to be found at the TNA in class E179, though some are held locally as parish officials retained a copy for their own use. They are arranged by parish, then present a list of tax payers and the number of hearths that they are liable to pay for. As with the rates, there is no indication where in the parish the property is, nor are the poorest householders listed as they were not liable to pay. That said, Essex Record Office has a list of returns for 1671 which include the names of those who were too poor to be chargeable. But they do give an accurate list of most of the householders in the parish and their approximate relative wealth. We can learn that Dr Brabourne had, from

1664 to 1672, a house with nine hearths in Northolt, whereas a neighbour John Winch had a house with only one chimney.

The number of names in these assessments varies enormously with the number of households in the parish. Greenwich parish assessments (available at Greenwich Local History Library) for 1662–4 include about 6,000 names, whereas those for Isleworth from 1664–74 number 960 and can be found at the Society of Genealogists' Library.

Some Hearth Tax assessments have been transcribed and so are easily available; but only for a few parishes. If your ancestors lived in Surrey, these have been transcribed and published; likewise for a number of Middlesex parishes, including Acton, Ealing, Harrow, Hanwell, Perivale, Staines and Northolt, as well as for a number of City parishes and the Kent parishes for 1662 have also been transcribed and indexed.

A useful list of what survives, and its whereabouts, can be found in J S Gibson, *The Hearth Tax and other later Stuart Tax Lists*.

Tithes

Since the Middle Ages, landowners and householders were obliged to pay tithes to the rector or vicar. These were goods; when the Revd Gold found himself in difficulties with his parishioners in Hayes in the early 1530s, it was over their presenting him with a tenth of the harvest crop. In 1836 the Tithe Commutation Act decreed that this payment should be in cash, and so each parish was assessed. Lists, known as apportionments, detailing landowners and tenants, with acreage, usage (arable, pasture, etc.) and value, were listed. What was even more valuable is that maps of each parish were made and so it is possible to locate where land was owned/rented. Three copies were made; one copy can be found at TNA (IR 29 is the series for apportionments, IR 30 for the maps), one at the LMA (in its role as diocesan record office) and one may be found at the local authority record office or sometimes parish churches retain them.

The Ship Tax

This was a form of taxation levied on several occasions during 1634–40 and is sometimes cited as a tax which was so unpopular that it led to the outbreak of hostilities between King and Parliament in 1642. Records are held at TNA, SP16 and 17. Essex Record Office has a transcript for the 1637 return, which has been indexed and lists 15,000 names. However, few assessments survive (there are none for Middlesex) and those which do are organized by county.

The Free and Voluntary Present

This was not 'what it says on the tin', but actually a list of about 130,000 people, with occupations, who gave money to the restored King Charles II in 1661. It is to be found in TNA, E179.

Window Tax

This was assessed from 1696–1851 on properties with six or more windows, being charged at 2 shillings per window. Collectors' assessment books exist for Finsbury and part of Clerkenwell for 1797–8 and 1807–8 at the LMA (TC). These list inhabitants and sums due. There are window tax assessments for Dagenham at Essex Record Office for 1785. Their existence is very partial indeed.

Game Duty

In 1784 and 1785, each person qualified to kill, hunt and sell game, such as gentlemen and gamekeepers, had to register with the clerk of the peace, who would issue a certificate in return for a fee. The clerk had then to transmit an annual account of certificates issued to the Commissioners of Stamp Duty. There are registers at the LMA for those in Middlesex from 1784 to 1808 and Westminster, 1799–1803. There is an alphabetical list for 1784–1807. Essex Record Office has registers for 1784–1806.

Poll Tax

It is often forgotten that the poll tax made a reappearance in the seventeenth century. Seven were raised in all, in 1660, 1667, 1678, 1689, 1691, 1694 and 1697. Records survive for the last four assessments. As ever, it was a tax on people, including both householders and lodgers, and sometimes, children, but exempting paupers. The records are to be found at TNA, in class E182, arranged by county, then by hundred, then by parish. The amount levied depended on the social status and occupation. The LMA has a transcribed copy of the assessment for the City for 1692.

The Land Tax

With the abolition of the Hearth Tax, the government, needing money to fight a war against France, imposed another tax. This commenced from 1692 and was maintained until 1963. As the name suggests, it was a tax on land and so, as with the rates, difficult to evade or avoid. It was levied at a certain number of shillings per £1 of the land's value. In wartime, it could rise to 4 shillings, but in peacetime was usually 1 or 2 shillings (often for political reasons). Surviving assessment lists for Middlesex, covering 1767 and 1780–1832 and for Westminster for 1767, 1781, 1797–1832 (but for two parishes also 1837–47) are at the LMA. For the City of London, their survival is even better – there are 522 volumes covering 1692–4 and 1703–1949, also at the LMA. Essex Record Office has assessments from 1780–1832, and those for 1782 have been indexed (there are 20,000 names). They also have lists of land tax payers for the Havering Hundred in 1692. Kent lists survive at the county record office from the 1720s. Some, however, exist at local authority record offices, with assessments for Hackney existing for 1727–1824 (with gaps) and 1939–49 at Hackney Archives. There are also some for Edmonton (1750) at Enfield Archives and for St George in the East (1801) at Tower Hamlets Archives. The reason why some Land Tax records do not survive is because until 1780 land tax records did not have to be returned to the clerk of the peace; afterwards they had to because they were needed for electoral purposes.

From 1798, landowners could pay a lump sum to indemnify them against later payments of this tax. The records can be found at TNA in the series IR23, which is arranged by county, then parish, then individual. It lists the landowners' tenants and contract number. Using this number, series IR24 can then be checked, which will give the acreage and where the owners lived. For redemptions paid from 1905 to 1950, series IR22 is the one to check.

Land Tax records are organized by parish, then, for an urban district, by street (but no street number is given.

We should also remember the Land Tax Redemption Office's Quotas and Assessments (TNA, IR23), which lists all property owners in England and Wales in 1798–9. Property owners are listed by parish.

Income Tax

This is the best known of taxes, introduced in 1798 to finance the war against Napoleon as a temporary expedient – but was long-lasting. It was abolished in 1802, to be reinstated in the following year. It was abolished again in 1816, with the end of hostilities, but was reimposed when Gladstone was Chancellor in 1842 and has remained with us since then. Until the early twentieth century it was only paid by the middle classes, who were obliged to complete annual tax returns until the introduction of PAYE after 1945. However, from our (genealogical) point of view, we can forget about it, because returns have not been retained. The exceptions are the returns for the parishes of St John's and St Margaret's, Westminster, for 1843–52 at the LMA, giving names, trades, profits and names of staff. Property and income tax assessment books for these parishes from 1837–47, 1853–4, 1856–7 can also be found at the LMA. These may have survived because they were duplicates. They were certainly not kept for statutory reasons.

Miscellaneous Taxes and Duties

There were a number of short-lived taxes. One was the Marriage Duty Tax, imposed from 1695 to 1706 on bachelors aged over 25 and childless widowers. There are lists of City taxpayers for 1695 (only) at the LMA.

Carriage duty was a tax imposed from 1747 to 1782, and lists of payers and defaulters can be found at TNA for 1753–66 at T47/2–4. Clearly those listed were those who were fairly wealthy, but if you believe your ancestor was among this happy number, it is worth taking a look at these sources. Likewise, lists of those paying servant tax in 1780 (the tax was introduced in 1777 and in force until 1852) can be found, arranged by county, then parish at TNA in class T47/8. Those not paying, or paying in arrears for 1777–1830 are listed in E182. There are also householders' returns for this tax for Clerkenwell residents for 1798–9 located at the LMA. Another tax for the late eighteenth century which was aimed at the better off in society was on hairpowder. Hairpowder duty registers for 1795–7 exist at Essex Record Office, giving names of payers of duty, arranged by parish, listing their occupations and status.

There were also a number of periodic subsidies levied by governments in the sixteenth and seventeenth centuries and records of some of those assessed for these survive. Many of these can be found in the TNA in class E179. Searches by place (but not person) for these can be made on the TNA website, www.nationalarchives.gov.uk/e179.

There is a list of subsidy payers of Westminster for 1625–45 at the Society of Genealogists' Library. Civil War assessments can exist, too, there being detailed lists of tax payers for 1641 and 1644 in the parishes making up the Hundred of Blackheath in *The Greenwich and Lewisham Antiquarian Society Transactions* of 1963.

Death Duties

From 1796, death duties became payable on estates as they passed from one owner on death to another. Until 1805, they only covered about a quarter of estates, but by 1857, all estates, unless valued at under £20, were included. If assets were valued at over £1,500, there would be a full reference. Many of the registers for the 1890s were burnt and, from 1903, there are none due to a new method of recording information, in files not registers, and these were destroyed thirty years after creation. The surviving records are at TNA, IR26, with an index in 1R27, and those from 1796–1811 are searchable by name online at TNA's website. Death duty registers show different information to wills; the latter show intent, these registers show what happened. They may also give information about the beneficiaries, addresses, the dates of birth, marriage and death of the deceased, family and other useful information.

As ever, tax records are more likely to exist for the wealthier members of society, but also serve as lists of most householders, except for the very poorest. The latter feature much less in these records than they do in others, such as the lists of those relieved with these rates and taxes, as mentioned in the previous chapter.

Chapter 6

EDUCATING LONDON

Schooling is now viewed in the Western world as a basic human right. All of this book's readers will recall their days at school and perhaps at other learning institutions, perhaps with fondness, perhaps not. This chapter will examine the records which may assist in learning about the education of your forebears.

Brief History of Education

First of all, it is worth giving a brief survey of the history of education in England. Youths have been instructed for centuries and such happened in London since at least the Middle Ages, almost always occurring within an ecclesiastical institution, and more for boys than girls. The institutions of church, state and manor all required men who could read and write and so could administer the activities of these increasingly technocratic and bureaucratic organizations. However, we know very little about any of these and next to nothing about those who were educated therein. This is because most were swept away during the Reformation of the mid-sixteenth century, as Protestantism was determined to uproot Catholicism, and their records were destroyed.

Yet the new order in church and state still needed administrators. New schools were set up, such as Harrow School founded by John Lyons in 1571, and older ones, such as Westminster, were refounded. Other public and grammar schools came into being from the sixteenth century onwards and many were located in London. Lesser schools also came into being, often financed by bequests left in wills. These were generally known as 'Charity Schools' and were at their height in the eighteenth century. Education was not compulsory and was mainly aimed at boys. Wealthy Catholic families usually sent their sons abroad to a Catholic country for their instruction (they were barred from attending English universities until the nineteenth century).

It was not until the nineteenth century that the state began to take an interest in the provision of education and to assist financially. In 1833 government grants were first forthcoming to help to provide schools.

These were known as National Schools, catering for the offspring of Anglicans, but there were also the British Schools for the children of Nonconformists. Private schools also flourished, but many were short-lived institutions, commercial ventures which closed when the master in charge retired, died or moved on for other reasons.

Although by the second half of the nineteenth century, most children living in London received some rudimentary education, attendance was not obligatory. Fees, however small, were often payable, and parents and employers often preferred children to be in paid employment rather than learning to read and write. But the needs of an increasingly industrial, commercial and democratic society meant that education was given even more importance. The Forster Education Act of 1870 decreed that schools should be built with public money in places which were lacking schools, or where existing provision was inadequate. These would be administered by elected school boards, in each parish. The new schools were known as 'Board Schools'. In 'The Adventure of the Naval Treaty', Sherlock Holmes waxes lyrical about them to Watson: 'Lighthouses, my boy! Beacons of the future! Capsules, with hundreds of bright little seeds in each, out of which will spring the wiser, better England of the future'. Many districts did not adopt school boards, because they believed that there were already enough private and church schools to cater for all children in the locality. Some church schools began to be administered and paid for by public money, though they often retained their original name. Most schools were for both sexes.

Elementary education until the age of 10 was made compulsory in 1880 and in 1902 the leaving age was raised to 12. In 1903 school boards were abolished and local councils took over the provision of education (in the LCC district the county council was alone responsible for education; in other counties it was shared between the county council and borough councils, the former being in charge of secondary education). Some children would proceed to secondary education at this age, but most would not. In 1918 the leaving age was raised to 14 and so secondary schools had to be built. These were usually single sex. After the Second World War, a new Education Act led to state education at secondary level being divided into three divisions: grammar, secondary modern and technical. The leaving age was raised to 15 years. In the 1960s and 1970s comprehensive education replaced the three-tier system, and one of the first comprehensive schools was at Eltham in the 1950s. Most grammar schools were obliged to become non-selective comprehensive schools.

Hackney schoolchildren, 1900s. Mrs Bignell's collection

Further education in London began with University College London in 1826 and King's College in 1829, swiftly becoming the University of London in 1836 and the third university in England to be founded. The University expanded over the following years, with other colleges such as Imperial, and the London School of Economics. The twentieth century led to further expansion of London University; Middlesex University, South Bank Polytechnic and others were founded. Until the late twentieth century, university attendance was only for a minority. It is also worth noting that evening classes for adults date from the late nineteenth century, known as Mechanics' Institutes, and courses were often administered by the University of London, and from the early twentieth century, by county councils and in more recent times, by borough councils.

All these institutions, especially from the later nineteenth century, created a vast amount of paperwork. Much of it dealt with the administration of the school/college, its courses and its finances. But some directly related to its pupils and staff and it is to these that we will now turn.

School Records

The most personal records created are school reports and examination certificates. These are given to pupils throughout their educational careers in order to help them and their parents and are often crucial for their further careers. Family historians should ensure that they and their family retain all of these as safely as possible. Unfortunately they are often lost or destroyed. The school records of my grandfather-in-law do not exist, but I count myself fortunate that some reports for my father-in-law do. In my professional capacity I have sometimes been asked by researchers if copies of such records exist and have to inform them that only one copy was made and, if that is lost, then nothing can be done to replace it. Copies of exam certificates can sometimes be purchased by application to the appropriate examination board if known.

School reports, of course, give a sentence or two for each subject a pupil studied. They might also give internal exam results and the pupil's place in the class. These reports were compiled at least once a year, perhaps termly in some cases. They can be very blunt and if a teacher thought that one of his charges was lazy or backward, would often say so, though towards the end of the twentieth century, such candid reports have been discouraged. These reports can also be glowing, but are usually mixed, with a pupil's strengths and weaknesses noted. As for exams, the key certificate before 1945 was the School Certificate, which was a statement of all-round achievement which should guarantee employment in the majority of cases. For the brightest of the bright, there was the Higher School Certificate, usually taken at 18 and an essential requirement for university entrance. After 1945, pupils were examined in a number of individual subjects, by numerous examination boards, with the Certificate of Secondary Education and the Ordinary Level exams, taken at 16, then the Advanced Level exams at 18. In 1987 the General Certificate of Education was introduced, though the A Levels were retained.

Sometimes report books for pupils do survive. At the LMA are report books for a number of City schools, such as those for the Aldersgate Ward School for 1885–1938 (ref. MS 1489). Lewisham Archives hold report books for the Haberdashers' Aske's School, Hatcham. But their survival is fairly unusual.

Schools also create other records which are of inestimable value to family historians. Attendance and admission/discharge registers are chief among these. However, they rarely survive in their entirety, and this comes as a shock to most researchers, who are horrified that records which relate to their ancestors could be destroyed or lost by the education authority or school, whose prime role should be surely to preserve these. Yet their loss could be because the school has ceased to exist, often due to amalgamation, or because space is limited and expensive, so anything which does not need to be kept for current or future use is in great danger of being removed in order to make way for what is needed. Sometimes such records may be deposited at the local authority archives, which will guarantee to keep them safely, or they can simply have been destroyed.

Where admission registers exist, they can be very useful indeed. They list the name of each pupil, with address, father's name (and sometimes occupation), the date of entry into the school, the date of discharge, and the reason for it, and often the previous school attended. Date of birth is usually stated. The pupils are listed in the books according to the date of admission, but there is often a name index at the beginning of each book, which makes searching so much easier. The admission register for the LCC School at Lancaster Road, for instance, records the following about Vera Page. She was born on 13 April 1921. Her father was Charles William Page, gas fitter of 4 Chapel Road. She was admitted to the school on 31 October 1928. Her last date of attendance was 14 December 1931. Of course, some of this information will be already known to the researcher – in my case, what was new was her date of admission to the school and her father's profession in 1928. If you know which school your ancestor attended, life is easier, but if you don't, the best course of action is to seek out the schools which were nearest to where they lived (as learnt from the census/directories/electoral registers). Since schools move or cease to exist, the use of a contemporary directory and map should help. Attendance registers list pupils and on which days they attended – or if they were late – but nothing else. They rarely survive.

The most common form of school record to survive are log books. Of the twenty-six schools for which records survive for the London Borough of Hillingdon, there are admission registers for four, attendance registers for three and log books for seven. Log books are often ignored by family historians. This is because it is extremely rare for them to mention any pupil by name. What they are is an account by the headmaster/headmistress of events in the school which are in any way exceptional. They might include a school inspection, a visit by a notable personality, a school trip, or evacuation and air-raid precautions during the Second World War, the school's celebratory events, such as Harvest Day or Empire Day, or closures due to holidays, elections or illness. However, for the family historian, they have two great uses.

Fancy dress display on Empire Day, Brentworth School, 1938. Author's collection

First, if your ancestor was a teacher, there will be references to him/her. These will include their appointment and first/last day at the school, possibly with reasons for departure. Any days of special leave granted, perhaps due to a death in the family or a training course, should be included. There is often a list of the school staff at the beginning of each year. Secondly, even if your ancestor was not a teacher, but you know that your ancestor was a pupil, you will learn about events at school which will have affected your ancestor and so know a little more about their schooldays.

There are two other important classes of record. First, there are the sinister-sounding 'Punishment Books'. These regulated physical chastisement in schools, chiefly from 1945 to the abolition of such punishment in the 1980s. They are arranged chronologically, giving pupil's name, reason for punishment, the number of strokes and who dealt these out. However, they only survive for a handful of schools and are usually closed for long periods of time.

Secondly there are school magazines. Grammar schools and private schools frequently had an annual school magazine, produced by staff and pupils. These included reports about the activities of the various

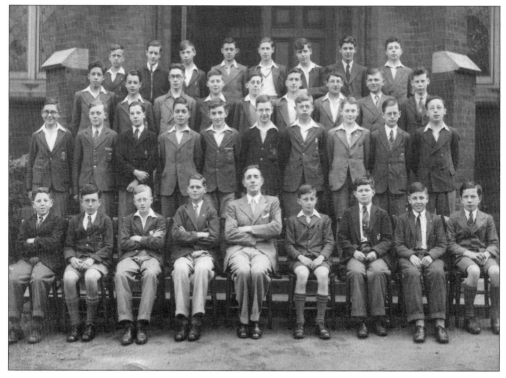

Stationers' School, c.1939. Mrs Bignell's collection

clubs, especially the sports clubs, and their achievements. Sometimes team photographs are included. Academic prowess is often noted, too, with lists of those who won places to university. There may be information about staff and about old pupils, too. Old Boy's/Girls' magazines also exist for those few schools which have such organizations. *The Old Stationers* is the magazine for former pupils of this livery school in Hornsey. There is information here about the activity of living former pupils, obituaries of those recently deceased, and reminiscences about the school.

School and college prospectuses might be worth mentioning, because they list courses and facilities offered, both educational and social. There should also be school pictures. However, these invariably give a positive impression of the school as they were meant to do.

The LCC was the education authority for the county of London after the abolition of the London School Board. Probably because of this, the survival of admission registers for the LCC schools is a lot better than for those in the MCC. LCC school records are to be found at the LMA and there are plans to digitalize these in the near future, so they will probably be available on ancestry.co.uk. The school records of the MCC, however, where they survive, are mostly with the local authority archives for the district in which the school was located. This may be because responsibility for education in the MCC was split between borough and county authorities, with the latter being responsible for the secondary schools only. Unfortunately, as noted, this has led to the patchy survival of school records for the MCC district. If the local authority archive does not have the records you want to see, contact the educational department of the local authority concerned, which may still have them (in Ealing's case, the admission registers for twenty schools were only deposited at the archives in 2008). If the school still exists, try contacting the headteacher. If all else fails, try the LMA, who do hold a very small number of MCC school records. There is a current scheme to digitalize MCC school admission registers for 1870–1914. School records may be closed for a certain number of years, depending on the sensitivity of the information contained therein.

We should not forget local newspapers, too. These often report school sports' days, school prize-giving events or any activity by the school which is unusual, for instance, a charitable event or sporting prowess. Exam results were once given in full, listing a school's pupils and the subjects in which they scored O and A level passes. These, of course, appear in the summer issues of the local newspaper.

Photographs of schools and schoolchildren/teachers often exist. These are doubly useful when the school in question does not survive, but also because they might show your ancestor. The LMA has a good collection of photographs of schools in the LCC area, and these can be seen in the search room there. Those for the now defunct Lancaster Road School show several of the children during special occasions, including a folk dance performed by them, and during Coronation celebrations in 1937. Local authority archives also have photographs of some of the schools in their jurisdiction, in various numbers.

It is probably worth mentioning poor law union and charity schools, which were often located outside the catchment area in which they took their pupils. The Central London District School at Hanwell catered for children from central London who were orphans or whose parents were unable to care for them (including, in the 1890s, Jack and Charles Chaplin). It existed from 1857 to 1933 and pupil admission registers and creed registers are located at the LMA. Yet pupil records of that for Marylebone in Southall do not exist. The City of London ran Christ's Hospital, a charity school for poor boys and girls from the sixteenth century and pupil records exist for 1563–1908 (for girls; for boys only from 1891–1908) and these are held at the LMA, as are those for the North Surrey Schools at Annerley, which took children from across London. Religious bodies also ran schools; such as the North Hyde Catholic school near Southall, but again pupil records rarely survive. Records of National Schools can be sometimes found in parish archives.

University Records

Many boys attended one of the colleges of Oxford or Cambridge from the Middle Ages to the present. There are a number of published registers of students, which are arranged alphabetically and give a short biography, including dates of matriculation and any degrees awarded, future career, birth and death dates, where born and perhaps father's name. Try J and J A Venn, *Alumni Cantabrigienses* for Cambridge and A B Emden, *Biographical register of the University of Oxford*, for the thirteenth century to 1540 and J Foster, *Alumni Oxonienses* for 1500–1886. Most graduates until the nineteenth century went on to enter the church, law or medicine. There are also registers for individual colleges, too, and *The Times* online lists names of those who graduated. Of course, others attended other universities, including those in Scotland and Leyden in the eighteenth century. Catholics were barred from British universities from the Reformation until the nineteenth century, so Catholic youths often went abroad, to France or Spain, for their education.

Then there is the University of London, founded in 1836 from King's College and University College, London. At the dawn of the twenty-first century, London University is the country's largest, with just over 135,000 students at its nineteen constituent colleges. As with the two older universities, student registers have been published. Contacting individual colleges is a useful tactic, for there may be more information available about former students than appears in the registers, though information about more recent students may be restricted, as in the case of schools.

Private Schools

As already noted, in the nineteenth and early twentieth century, there were a great number of private schools in and around London. Many were very small and left no record, save for adverts in the local press and entries in directories. Even well-established ones, with some

Haberdashers' Aske's School, New Cross, 1900s. Author's collection

renown – the Great Ealing School was attended, amongst others, by W S Gilbert, John Henry Newman and Thomas Huxley, for instance – failed to leave any corpus of records. Likewise, Mr Valentine's select boys' school on Blackheath in the late nineteenth century folded when Valentine retired and records were disposed of. Yet if the school was a boarding school, and your ancestor was there in census year, you will find them listed there. Of course, this does not tell you when they entered the school, left or with what, if any, distinctions. Yet it is better than nothing. Records of former private schools, where they exist, tend to be with the local authority archives.

These are rather different to those of the state schools. Where schools still exist, such as Harrow, Westminster, Dulwich and Highgate, for example, this is usually straightforward. A researcher should first check that there are published lists of former pupils – as there are for Harrow and Westminster from the eighteenth century, and for Dulwich from 1858–1926. These can be found on the open shelves of the TNA library for instance and should always be consulted prior to contacting a particular school. Many published lists of alumni are to be found at the Society of Genealogists' Library, too, along with school histories. These lists are arranged in chronological order, and there is usually an index. They give details of home and parents, school career and subsequent career details and (perhaps) death. However, many pupils normally lived far from London.

There were also special schools in London aimed at particular groups. Lewisham Archives have the records of the Congregational School, for sons of Congregational ministers, and the Royal Naval School, for sons of naval officers.

Children from London might be educated at a school outside London, of course. From the early nineteenth century, clergymen's sons often attended Radley School in Oxfordshire. Among them was Maurice Odell Tribe, son of the vicar of St Anne's church, Brondesbury, between 1907 and 1911. These mini-biographies of pupils would usually exclude anything discreditable – that for the said Tribe neglects to mention that he later shot his sister dead and then committed suicide, for instance.

The Inns of Chancery and of Court

Although civil law was taught at Oxford and Cambridge from the Middle Ages, they did not teach common law until the mid-nineteenth century. Any youth wanting to be a solicitor could attend a number of Inns of Chancery in London from the Middle Ages until their extinction in the nineteenth century. These were preparatory schools for lawyers. Unfortunately pupil lists for only four of at least a dozen have survived. Records survive at TNA (Clement's Inn), the Library of the Middle Temple (New Inn). The Law Society (Staple Inn) and those for Barnard's Inn have been published by the Selden Society in 1995.

Would-be barristers had to spend seven to eight years at one of the Inns of Court (until the 1840s), these four being Gray's Inn, Lincoln's Inn, the Middle Temple and the Inner Temple. After the 1840s, university graduates served three years, and from the 1960s, two years. Numbers, too increased, with 230 barristers practising in 1780 and 11,000 in the first decade of the twenty-first century. Admission registers exist for all four Inns. Many have been published and so are relatively easily available: Middle Temple (1501–1975), Inner Temple (1547–1850 available on a database), Gray's Inn (1521–1889) and Lincoln's Inn (1420–1893). All these courts have libraries which have much other information, too. Lawyers will be discussed further in Chapter 7.

The Apprenticeship System

Apart from schools and colleges, there was another once common method of educating youths, which was particularly prevalent in the seventeenth and eighteenth centuries. This was the system of apprenticeship. A master of a trade was paid to take a youth to serve under him in order that the young man would learn the business on the job. He would enter into a formal contract with his master usually when aged 14, but possibly as young as 12, and would normally serve seven years. He would work in return for pocket money and board and lodgings. The lot of apprentices varied considerably, as Hogarth's painting of the idle and the industrious apprentices shows – the former ends up on the gallows, the second ends up marrying his master's daughter.

This system began following the Statute of Apprentices of 1563, which forbade anyone entering a trade who had not served the said apprenticeship. This legislation remained in force, with modifications, until 1814. Stamp duty was payable on the indentures of apprenticeship from 1710. These survive in the form of apprenticeship books and are held at TNA (IR 1). These include lists of articled clerks. They are arranged geographically (for London, see the 'City' registers), and then roughly chronologically. They list the name, address and trade of the master, the name of the apprentice and the date of the indenture. Sometimes the names of the apprentice's parents are also given.

Some apprentices enlisted in the armed forces, contrary to the terms of their apprenticeship indentures, and once this was discovered, they were returned to their masters. Lists of these youths for 1806–35 can be found in TNA, WO 25/2962. Yet there were military and naval apprenticeships; for boys from the Royal Naval Asylum at Greenwich and at the Duke of York's Military School, Chelsea (many were orphans, often the sons of former sailors or soldiers). They can be found in TNA, WO 143/52, covering 1806–48 and in ADM 73/421–48, covering 1808–38, respectively. There were also apprenticeships in the Merchant Navy from 1823, too. For London, these can be found in TNA, BT 150/1–14 (covering 1824–79) and BT 150/47–57 (covering 1880–1953). These give details of the apprentice's name, age, date, terms of apprenticeship and his master's name. From 1880 they also give the port at which he first signed on.

The Watermen and Lightermen's Company were responsible for traffic on the Thames from the sixteenth to the twentieth century and many of their employees were previously apprentices. The LMA has the apprentice binding books for 1688–1908 (MS 6289) and the apprentice affidavit books, 1759–1897 (MS 6291). These give the apprentice's name, the date and place of baptism, the date he began his apprenticeship and the date he became a free waterman, as well as naming his master. Older entrants into the profession had an apprenticeship of only two years, and their admissions, 1865–1926, are covered in MS 19548A.

However, many apprenticeships were exempt from the stamp duty already mentioned and so do not appear in these registers. These would include children apprenticed by charities or by parish vestries. Vestry minute books refer to children of poor parents, or orphans, who the parish paid to have apprenticed and so no longer be a burden on the parish rates. There may be additional references to the apprentice if there was trouble – Hanwell Vestry investigated a case where it was alleged that a master had ill used his apprentice and the steps taken against the master to try and ensure it would not recur. One charity which paid to apprentice children was Thomas Coram's Foundling Hospital. The LMA has registers of apprentices which are accessible from 1751–1891 (A/FH/A12/003/001–3). These are indexed alphabetically. JPs also authorized the apprenticeships of poor children; minutes of the Blackheath JPs are to be found at the Greenwich History Centre.

Apprentices sometimes found themselves in trouble with the law. The Middlesex Quarter Sessions refers to apprentices in dispute with their masters. Pepys makes reference in the later 1660s to apprentices being involved in riots; and they were said to be prominent in the anti-Catholic rioting in London in 1688. It may be worth checking criminal records, if your ancestor was an apprentice, therefore. It should also be stated that it is estimated that about half of those who began apprenticeships in London failed to complete them.

Most surviving school records do not concern individual pupils, if records survive at all. Very few education records survive before the late nineteenth century except for those of the universities, some private schools and the inns of court. For the twentieth century there is a better chance of their existing, but even then, only for a minority of cases. Often records only survive for part of the time that the school existed. Yet it is another sphere which a researcher should investigate.

Chapter 7

SOCIAL AND CULTURAL LONDON

O ur London ancestors were born, went to school (perhaps), worked, got married (probably), had children (probably) and went to church or chapel (probably). They may have been involved in war, they almost certainly paid taxes and they may have arrived in London from another country. They died. But their lives contained other activity and we shall explore how to find out about this, by examining leisure pursuits, sickness and poverty, in that order.

Leisure Pursuits

In the past, working hours were longer than they are now. It was only in the Victorian era that the Ten Hour Act came into force, limiting adult working hours to that number per day (Sunday was almost always a day of leisure). It is also worth noting that, until at least the early twentieth century, homes were where people slept and ate, but were not primarily where they spent their leisure hours. Recreational activity before the nineteenth century is difficult to pinpoint. We can certainly generalize: cricket and football were played, though not in forms recognizable to us, cock fighting, bear baiting and theatre were popular, as were attendance at concerts and watching or participating in trials of physical strength. Drinking in the many pubs – 'the poor persons' club' as G K Chesterton called them – in London was another. Dr Johnson remarked, 'there is nothing which has yet been contrived by man, by which so much happiness is produced as by a good tavern or inn'. If you find the names of the pubs near to where your ancestor lived, you will know which drinking dens they probably patronized. Licensing records, incidentally, can be found at the appropriate county record office; at the LMA, those for Middlesex are at MR/LV and those for Westminster are at WR/LV. They are arranged chronologically, giving date of licence/renewal, licence holder, name of pub and when awarded. In the seventeenth and eighteenth centuries, coffee houses were popular and

London nightlife, c.1900. Author's collection

in the nineteenth there were even temperance houses in which working men could enjoy non-alcoholic beverages.

It was in the nineteenth century when organized activities began to be more common. Clubs and societies for sporting, intellectual, political and other activities sprang into being, especially as the century progressed. These were often led by the local elite, who are easily identifiable. Lady Mosley, mother to Sir Oswald, was the president of the Greenford Horticultural Society in the 1920s, for instance. Active membership of clubs and societies probably peaked in the early twentieth century, when working hours had fallen, income for many had risen and before the rival attraction of television became the mass medium of entertainment in the 1960s and onwards.

There are several sources for the membership of such organizations. First there are the records of the clubs themselves. The club may have produced an annual or monthly journal, chronicling its activities. The Ealing Microscopical and Natural History Society, whose records exist for 1877–1934, listed its members and the society's officers in its publication. Among the members were Maurice Hulbert, a councillor, and Charles Jones, a well-known local surveyor. If your ancestor belonged to such a club, you can trace the years in which he was listed and if you are lucky you may find he made a more active contribution to club life by giving a paper, leading an expedition, being a committee officer and so forth. For some clubs, however, such records are not made systematically. The Ealing Ladies' Hockey Club, founded in about 1888, only has a list of members with addresses for the 1960s. However, the minute books (surviving from 1930) list the club's officers and the AGM minutes list who attended these meetings (including Violet Grey, a secret agent). Likewise the Acton Chrysanthemum, Dahlia and Flora Art Club only has membership records for the 1980s. The Hayes and Harlington Arts Club has only the minutes from 1962–71 and correspondence 1965–70 to show for itself. As always, if your ancestor was a prominent member of a society, then they are more likely to be recorded in club archives.

Then there are newspapers. Newspapers record significant happenings in the life of clubs and societies. They are particularly interested in sport, especially football and cricket, because newspaper editors assume that this is what interests their readership. If your

Programme for the Southgate Philanthropic Society Annual Dinner, 1930. Mrs Bignell's collection

ancestor was a member of a local football, rugby or cricket team, then expect to see his name appear in the local press on a regular basis in the given season. Often there were blow-by-blow accounts of cricket games, as when an Uxbridge team played a Clapton one in 1863. There may even, in the twentieth century, be pictures of ancestors and their team-mates. Lists of teams are usually given in each match report, as well as the names of the goal scorers/wickets takers. Although these sports dominate the sports page of the local newspapers, athletics, golf, hockey, skittles and tennis will also feature therein. Annual dinners and social events, and even AGMs, of clubs and societies were often reported locally and the prominent club members usually mentioned. Non-sports' events can also appear. Detailed lists of entrants at flower and garden festivals can be found in the pages of the *Middlesex County Times* for 1892, for instance.

Finally there are the ephemera which clubs often produce. Amateur dramatics clubs, for example, produce theatre programmes, which list the cast and others involved in productions. There may be team photographs or even official histories of the club, especially if it reached its centenary. Clubs which had a longer history, or even still exist, are usually more likely to have surviving archives. The problem, of course, is knowing which team/society (if any) your ancestor belonged to. Older family members may recollect that grandfather Tom played football for his work's team, but if you don't know this, you must decide whether it is worth trawling through newspapers and club minutes/membership lists in the hope of locating anything. Much will depend on priorities and time available.

London was also home to many other clubs, mostly situated around Pall Mall and Piccadilly, catering for the upper middle classes and above, as a London Guide of 1927 noted, 'Admission . . . is almost entirely a matter of social status'. Most were formed in the nineteenth century, such as The Carlton for Conservatives, The Reform Club for Liberals, the United University Club, the United Services Club for officers, the Explorers' and many others. Of course these clubs were national in scope, but being based in London had a more than proportionate membership from London. These provided members with a home from home; dining and accommodation as well as being a place to meet with like-minded souls. Some of these still exist and may be worth contacting if you believe your ancestor was a member.

We should not forget that political membership was far greater in the first half of the twentieth century. Political parties had numerous clubs and societies. Archives of such, and their magazines, may list ancestors. These, for local associations and constituency parties are held by local authority record offices, rather than the national headquarters of such organizations, who maintain national records.

Another major type of club was the Freemasons, often viewed in the media and fiction as sinister secret societies. In fact, the authorities in the 1790s saw them as anything but. They were viewed as charitable societies. However, each lodge had to register with the magistrates and send annual certificates of members. At the LMA, you can view certificates for the Middlesex lodges, 1799–1888 (MR/SF) and those for the Westminster ones, 1799–1805 (WR/SF), which give names of members, occupation, address and name of lodge. Other county record offices should also hold similar material where it survives.

Friendly Societies flourished in the nineteenth century and early twentieth century. These were benefit clubs, where working people would pay a weekly sum, and at times of sickness or death could claim a dividend to help them through difficult times. They had to register with the magistrates, too, but the county record offices only tend to have records of registration, not membership details. Surviving lists and other records pertinent to members may be found at local record offices.

Youth movements began in Britain in the later nineteenth century, such as the Church Lads' Brigade and the Boys' and Girls' Brigades. These often had a religious basis. Scouting, which began in 1907, aimed more at promoting good citizenship and outdoor values. These organizations kept records of activities and members. There may also be photographs, as exist for the 10th Hackney Scout Group for 1914–53 (located at Hackney Archives). As with political archives, seek either the appropriate local record office or the organization itself, not the national headquarters.

Archives for sports and other clubs are principally to be found in the local authority record offices for the district to which they relate. As always, if the particular club survives to this date, try contacting them, too.

We should also remember that employers often organized social and sporting activities for their workforces, especially if employees were numerous (churches also organized such activities, too). Newspapers reported annual employees' days out to the seaside or countryside, as well as Christmas parties and annual balls. Company brochures also mention these events and may mention individuals by name.

As with public houses, a popular leisure pursuit at least up until the 1950s, was the cinema, with some people going several times weekly.

79th North London Air Scouts headed notepaper, 1943. Mrs Bignell's collection

Londoners also went to exhibitions, such as the Great Exhibition in Hyde Park in 1851 and then to the Crystal Palace near Sydenham in later decades. Museums and art galleries were patronized by many, too. It is also worth mentioning that, from at least the sixteenth century, London has been the national capital of prostitution, and many men followed James Boswell's example when he was in London in 1762–3. Football and cricket matches, as well as the University boat race on the Thames, attracted and still attract many thousands of people. From the late nineteenth centuries, the free libraries have been popular with many people, and from the 1930s most homes had a wireless, as home entertainment began to make itself felt. Parks and open spaces in London, such as Hyde Park, Richmond Park and Hampstead Heath also accord opportunities for spending leisure hours. On 22 February 1664 Samuel Pepys wrote, 'Thence to take a turn in St. James' Park; and meeting Anthony Joyce, walked with him a turn into Pell Mell.' There is much for the spectator to enjoy, sometimes for free, in London. However, as with the myriad pub-goers mentioned earlier, these activities rarely leave any mark in written history unless through diaries or reminiscences.

Ill-Health

Everyone becomes ill at some time in their lives. Some will require hospital treatment. There have been hospitals in London since the Middle Ages, principally St Thomas' and St Bartholomew's and later Bethlehem (Bedlam) which catered for the insane. There were other hospitals, mostly being part of monastic foundations, but these were suppressed in the Reformation of the sixteenth century. The eighteenth century saw the establishment of a wave of hospitals, including Thomas Guy's in 1725, Thomas Coram's Foundling Hospital of 1739 and the Greenwich Seaman's Hospital, and a number of other specialist hospitals in the capital (including that at Chelsea for aged soldiers). It was not until the later nineteenth century, with the growth of outlying towns, that hospitals sprang up outside central London. Workhouses also had an infirmary attached. Then there were the 'cottage hospitals', relatively small buildings, either purpose-built or converted from existing premises. These primarily catered for patients who could not afford medical care and for whom moving any distance would have been dangerous. Surbiton had a cottage hospital by the 1870s, as did Ealing and Richmond.

All these hospitals (except the workhouse infirmaries) were privately managed and maintained. They relied on donations and subscriptions from residents and from funds garnered by special events, such as carnivals. Hanwell Carnival began as a method of helping to pay for the parish's cottage hospital. Medical staff would mostly be made up of honorary physicians; local doctors who gave up part of their week to work on cases there which suited their specialism. In 1948, the National Health Service was born and almost all of these existing hospitals were simply turned over to public ownership and control, though as decades went by, many of the smaller ones were amalgamated and the original buildings demolished or turned to a new role.

These pre-1948 hospitals directly concerned, therefore, not only patients and staff (paid and otherwise), but those people who voluntarily contributed time and money to support them. Without their support, they simply could not have survived. A hospital committee was usually responsible for raising money and this they did in several ways. People could give an annual sum, or could give irregularly. Collection tins were often found in workplaces, shops and schools. There was also an annual fête to raise money. Lists of those who gave money, with the amount by their name, were often published in the hospital's annual reports, which also listed the honorary surgeons, but not patients. The Great Hall of St Bartholomew's Hospital, lists thousands of subscribers' names in gold all around the walls, dating from the sixteenth century to 1905.

The major form of patient records that these hospitals produced were admission and discharge books and registers of operations. These are sometimes indexed by patients' names, but otherwise the names are arranged in date order of entry to the hospital and the operation. Name, address, date of arrival and operation are usually listed, with date of discharge or death, and the name of the operating surgeon usually appears therein. However, there is a general closure period of 100 years on such confidential information, from the time of the last date in the said register, in order to protect patient confidentiality. People wanting to check their own details can usually be given that information (though not access to the register itself) upon application to the custodians of the registers and to the hospital which created those records. In some cases there may be a fee payable to staff to search registers on a researcher's behalf. However, in the case of the LMA, the infirmary records of workhouses (as opposed to records of hospitals per se) are only subject to a sixty-five-year closure period; so all these (up to 1930 when workhouses were no longer managed by poor law unions) are open to public inspection, whereas

London Hospital, 1900s. Author's collection

those in the 1910s/1920s for other hospitals, for example, St Thomas', are not.

There is a website, 'Hospital records', created by the Wellcome Institute for the History of Medicine and hosted by TNA (www.nationalarchives. gov.uk/hospitalrecords/). It can be searched by name of hospital, and for each one, it gives an administrative history and a list of the records held, with their whereabouts. Having looked at some pages of this site, and after seeing an impressive listing, the author was disappointed to note that, in the instance of Perivale Maternity Hospital, there was a footnote to record that the current whereabouts of the hospital records was unknown – meaning that almost certainly they have been destroyed or lost.

Archives of older hospitals are usually open. Those for the British Lying-In Hospital in Holborn include patient registers for 1749–1868. The hospital was for wives of servicemen and poor married women prior to their giving birth. The mother's name and dates of admission/discharge/death are given, as is the child's name and date of birth, and the father's name, occupation and whereabouts. These can be viewed on microfilm at TNA. From 1849, place and date of marriage is also noted. The records can be see online at bmdregisters.com.

There were other hospitals, too, which were funded out of county rates. Asylums for the mentally ill were founded in Middlesex in the nineteenth century. These were initially designed for the pauper insane. The first was the County Asylum at Southall, usually (and erroneously) called the Hanwell Asylum. This was built in 1829–31 and expanded over the decades, so that by the end of the nineteenth century, there were about 3,000 inmates in this enclosed community. Another large asylum was at Colney Hatch, in 1851. As with hospitals, admission and discharge books are the main class of records which are of interest to the family historian, with patients' name, address, occupation, date of birth and date of entry and they also state what the patient is suffering from, and what the treatment was. They may record any previous institution the patient had attended and to which subsequent one they were sent. There also may be references to a patient's condition at regular intervals, as in the case of Aaron Kominski, who has been suspected of being Jack the Ripper. These records are usually closed for 100 years, too.

Private asylums also existed around London. These were for those whose friends and relations could pay fees. They tended to be small-scale institutions, dealing with numbers in single or double figures. Dr John Conolly (1794–1866), who had been superintendent of the County Asylum mentioned in the paragraph above, opened his own private asylum in Hanwell, which he ran for two decades, and a mile west of the county asylum was Southall Park, which was run as a private asylum in 1838–83. However, records do not survive of these, and only the census returns will list patients, and then, often by initials only.

The main problem with hospital records is that you need to know where your ancestor might have been treated. If they were there on census night, then you can work backwards from that date in order to find them in the admission and creed registers. Otherwise, as with workhouse registers, it is potentially a long slog.

Most London hospital archives, though by no means all, are held at the LMA; some are held by local authority archives. Richmond Royal Hospital archives are held at Surrey History Centre, for instance. Many archives which are relevant to patients do not exist, especially for the early decades of the hospital's existence. Many workhouse infirmary registers held at the LMA are available online at ancestry.co.uk, though these are not complete at time of writing and cannot be yet searched by name; instead a chronological search is required. Yet this saves a visit to the LMA, so is a valuable asset.

The Poor

As has been noted in Chapter 4, from the sixteenth century to 1834 the care of the poor was the lot of the parish. However, in 1834, the New Poor Law Act was passed. This was in order to provide for a more standardized and rational administration for the relief of the poor. Poor law unions, each made up of a number of parishes, were formed throughout the country. In Middlesex in 1894 there were six unions, each made up of a different number of parishes. Each union was administered by a board of guardians, men (and women after 1875) who were elected by the ratepayers. They were financed out of the poor rates, which were paid in the same fashion as the rates under the Old Poor Law, as has already been explained in Chapter 4, only this time they went to a different payee. Another major change was the building of a workhouse per union. In these places, paupers could receive what was termed 'indoor relief' (the old parish system had been a form of outdoor relief, with relief being paid whilst the paupers remained in their own home). Each workhouse was presided over by a master and a mistress (often a married couple), and included an infirmary and chapel. Outdoor relief tended to be given far less than it had before. The system continued until 1929, when the county councils took over responsibility for the poor and the workhouse hospitals were often turned into the public hospital for the district, as occurred in Lewisham.

People went to the workhouses for the same reasons as they would have claimed outdoor relief from the parish. That is, they were unable to support themselves financially, perhaps due to illness or old age, perhaps due to pregnancy or extreme youth. Workhouses have a bad reputation, in part because of the opening chapters of Dickens's *Oliver Twist*. It is certainly true that conditions therein could be harsh and the food drab.

These unions created a mass of documentation. However, although most of the unions began in 1836, for many of them there are very few records about individuals in the early decades. Rather, it is the minutes and the accounts which have survived for these years. For most unions, the key records for inmates only exist from the 1870s to 1929 (or for even more selective date ranges). These records are the admission and discharge registers and the creed registers.

These will give the name, occupation, parish and age of the pauper, when they were admitted and when discharged, the cause of admittance/discharge, and, in the creed registers, the religion of the pauper. For instance, the admission register for the Islington Workhouse on Cornwallis Road notes that, on Monday 13 December 1897, Edith Reed, a 26-year-old laundress, from Islington and being of the Church of England, was admitted to the workhouse. Sometimes several members of a family would enter at the same time, perhaps a mother and children. In some cases, the reason for admittance is given, such as 'temporary disability'. If only we could know more.

For most of London, these records are held at the LMA; some can be found at local authority archives. They can be viewed at the LMA on microfilm. Some of them (those for fifteen unions in London) can also be viewed online at ancestry.co.uk, and though they are not indexed, this at least saves a visit to the LMA to view microfilm. These are all arranged in date order, in the order that a pauper was admitted into the workhouse. However, in some cases, there is a manuscript index of those whose names are entered in the book, so that is helpful. Even so, unless you know that an ancestor was admitted into a particular workhouse (perhaps because they were there on census night), or died in one, then searching blindly can, as always, be a lengthy and not necessarily productive task. Paupers were sometimes, though not always, admitted to the workhouse for the union of the parish in which they dwelt.

Workhouse records can also include lists of youths being apprenticed, with name, date of indenture, age, parents' names (if known – and alive), to whom they were assigned, their trade and address. Some kept registers of children resident there. Workhouses maintained the mentally ill, too, listing name, when admitted, age, previous residence and date of death/discharge.

References to inmates may also be found in other records. They may be mentioned by name in the minute books, perhaps because they were the subject of a complaint or breach of regulations. If you do find that your ancestor entered a workhouse, it may also be worth reading about life there, perhaps finding out what the diet and conditions were like. The website www.workhouses.org.uk contains much which is relevant.

Orphanages and Children's Homes

Children often ended up in workhouses, as did the fictional Oliver Twist. But this was not the inevitable destination of orphaned or abandoned children. There were numerous charitable institutions in London which would take children on board, to clothe, feed and house them. Most also aimed to provide the children with training in some form of useful occupation which would befit their lowly status; for girls this was usually domestic service (the largest single employer of women in nineteenth-century Britain). Some were founded by religious organizations, others by secular charities. The most famous are the Barnardo's Homes, founded by Dr Thomas Barnardo, in Stepney in 1867; the last one closed in 1981. The location of their records is given in the Bibliography.

Dealing with enquiries about ancestors who were in children's homes is the frequent lot of most archivists in the employ of local authorities. Unfortunately, the records of most of these organizations do not exist. This is because most were small-scale and local, and once they closed down, as many did in the mid-twentieth century, all the records they created were disposed of, too. Although information about the institution may exist elsewhere, especially in local newspapers, perhaps when there was a fête or open day, or an important visitor, this will not name individual inmates.

It should be noted that adoption was not formalized in law until 1927 and prior to that date other family members often took a child whose parents had died into their care. An exhaustive study of the topic is Georgina Stafford's *Where to Find Adoption Records*. Some children were given different surnames on adoption and this can make identification difficult.

Charities

As with the hospitals before 1948, there were a great number of private secular charities which sought to alleviate poverty. These began to appear from the sixteenth century and many were benefactions by individuals, who bequeathed land, property or investments, the interest or rent to be used by trustees to benefit the objects of that charity. These were often children or poor widows. More substantial charities might result in the foundation of schools or almshouses. The latter were sometimes administered by organizations, such as the City's livery companies. The Goldsmith's Company founded an almshouse in Acton in 1811 for instance, for a small number of elderly people. Charity minute books often name those who were being relieved (and those who were refused), the reason for such relief and the amount given. Often priority was given to those who had lived in a particular place for a long time, if they were of good moral character (the deserving poor) and sometimes if they were of a particular trade or religion.

You may also find that your ancestor was involved on 'the other side' of charity, too. I recently found that my late father-in-law's maternal grandfather, William Howard, was chairman of the Southgate Philanthropic Society. These societies often kept records, including minute books and accounts, listing committee members, and their activities were often chronicled in the local press. They held social events for their members and the annual dinner dance listed the music which was played for dancing, the toasts which were made and the food they ate.

Dr Johnson famously remarked that 'When a man is tired of London he is tired of life, for there is in London everything that a man could desire'. Londoners are spoilt for choice, whether they want to engage in activity or as spectators, whether alone or as part of a crowd. Many of these pastimes are, for individuals, unrecorded, but some are not. On a darker note, there are few people who have not had to visit a hospital and many readers will have ancestors who needed to stay temporarily in a workhouse.

Chapter 8

BUSINESS AND WORKING LONDONERS

One of the principal reasons why people live in or near London is employment (that is certainly my reason). As capital city, London is also the centre for the headquarters of major public- and private-sector organizations which are large employers. There is also a significant service sector of restaurants and theatres, and other places of entertainment. Historically London was a great industrial and trading city, too, though this is less so now. The streets of London are not paved with gold, but money is an important facet of Londoners' relationship with their city. This chapter therefore, looks at how to find out about our ancestors' working lives. Having learnt what their occupations were by the census and by parish registers and/or civil registration certificates, the researcher can then look for further information. This chapter deals with civil professions; military ones are dealt with in Chapter 10.

The Professions

It is easiest of all to trace your ancestor's career if he or, in the twentieth century and onward, she, belonged to one of the professions. There were more from the professions in London proportionately because that is where the headquarters of many organizations which employed them were located. You may already have details of their education, garnered through school and university sources, as already explained in Chapter 6, and army officers are dealt with in Chapter 10. Doctors, lawyers, headteachers and clergymen are all easy to track down in published sources. The *Law List* from 1775, the *Medical Register* from 1859 and the *Medical Directory* from 1845, and *Crockford's*, from 1858 were and are all produced regularly, often on an annual basis. *The Clergy List* from 1841 and *The Church Directory and Almanac* from 1900 should also be mentioned because the former predates *Crockford's* and the latter was published during the Second World War, which *Crockford's* was not. We should also note G Hennessey's *Novum Repertorum Ecclesiasticum*

Parochiale Londiense, covering London clergy for 1321–1898, which is indexed. Similar yearbooks exist for Catholic priests and Nonconformist ministers, schoolmasters, architects, dentists, actuaries and others. They are organized in alphabetical order by surname, though often within subsections – medical listings in the nineteenth century are divided into two sections ('London' and 'Country'), whereas the *Law Lists* have different sections for barristers, London solicitors and provincial lawyers. They give the age, address, educational and career history of the professional; retired members are also included. When names cease to appear, they are probably dead. For instance, in the *Law List* of 1888, one Montague John Druitt (sometimes suspected of being Jack the Ripper) is listed, but not in the one for the next year (he died in December 1888). His entry reads:

> Druitt, M.J. I [Inner Temple] 29 Apr. 1885, 9 King's Bench Walk, Temple EC, sp. pl. [special pleader] West Country Circ. Hants., Portsmouth and Southampton Sess [ions].

Details for doctors and clergy are often even more extensive. The London section of the *Medical Directory* for 1942 gives, for Dr John Horace Dancy, his address, telephone number, medical qualifications, with dates and places, educational details and a summary of the medical posts held, together with the fact that he had once served as a captain in the RAMC.

Once you have traced your ancestor by these lists, it may be sensible to carry on looking through the series of these volumes as far as you can in both directions, learning more information (and seeing much of the same, too) as you proceed. Significant runs of these volumes can be found at the LMA, TNA and the Guildhall Library.

Directories will also list these people, perhaps in both the 'Court' and 'Business' sections. They are more likely to have obituaries (for dates of death see death certificates or wills) in the local press as they are often significant figures in the local community. Until at least the 1960s, local newspapers carried much church news, so if your ancestor was a clergyman and you know his parish (from *Crockford's*), this could be a useful source of information; you can also check parish magazines (which are monthly), for there is usually an address from the vicar therein. Newspapers often had adverts for private schools, giving details of the curriculum, fees, when the school was established, and so on. Clergymen were often schoolmasters, too; in the eighteenth century, the Revd William Dodd ran a boys' school in Ealing as well as being a royal chaplain (and a forger).

There are other sources. For clergy, ordination papers for the diocese are held at the LMA, and the ongoing clergymen's database (www.kcl.ac.uk/humanities/cch/cce/), aiming to cover all Anglican clergy from 1536 to 1834, may also be worth a look, though the London diocese is not yet included. For lawyers of the nineteenth and twentieth centuries, contact the Law Society who, for a fee, may be able to supply further details.

Shopkeepers

Directories will list these in the business sections, of course. But to learn more about your greengrocer ancestor, you could look at the local newspapers, which carried adverts for some of the local shops, and these give a good flavour of shopkeeping at that time. For instance, in the *Southall News* of April 1886, which, as with most newspapers until the early twentieth century, carried adverts on the front page, we learn that Mrs Neave ran a stationers and booksellers shop on 6 Southall High Street. In detail, she boasted of 'Monthly Magazines and Weekly Periodicals supplied on the day of publication', with 'Daily papers delivered at 8 am' and she also sold 'Christmas, Birthday & New Year's cards' and 'Stationery of every description'. Meanwhile, G Lowe of Hortus, Southall, advertised the fact that he sold 'seed potatoes' and 'Garden seeds of the best Quality at moderate prices'. Some shopkeepers listed a few of their goods with quantities and prices. Ephemera collections at local authority archives may have something relevant to the business and museums may have examples of packaging or other items from long-gone shops. Local authority archives also have photograph collections; there may be a picture of the shop amongst them; sometimes with the proud proprietor standing outside. They probably will not have anything regarding your ancestor's business, but ask, for you have nothing to lose. Chambers of Commerce existed in many suburbs and published annual journals which included lists of members, which included shopkeepers, and adverts for some of them therein, too, and these volumes can often be found in local authority archives. In some cases, these organizations may still exist and could be contacted directly.

Business Records

It is always easier to learn about the man at the top than his clerks and labourers. Senior figures in the business world are usually allotted obituary columns in the local and sometimes national press. But what about the majority of employees? Tracking them down is often a matter of luck. Some business archives do survive, but many tend to be account books, minutes of board meetings, advertising material, product details and so forth, all of which help give an impression about the company, but may say little about employees – as with school log books.

Some local authority archives have excellent holdings of business archives. One is Hackney Archives. They have staff records for A Norman & Sons, footwear wholesalers of Shoreditch, from 1941–60, and for Berger, Jenson & Nicholson, paint manufacturers of Homerton, from 1831–94 (with gaps), as well as those for the well-known match manufacturers, Bryant & May Ltd, covering 1852–1960, and for other local firms, too. However, staff records only survive for a very few firms.

Businesses often took out insurance on their property and goods. Several insurance firms sprang up in the later seventeenth century, partly as a response to the Great Fire of 1666. Their archives can provide useful information about businesses, although of course, they also covered domestic property. In some cases, the business was run from the owner's house. The information given in the following sets of registers usually includes the number of the policy, the name/location of the agent, name, status, occupation and address of the policy holder, location of the premises, type and nature of the property, its value, the premium paid and when the renewal was due. Details of any tenants might also be given, if applicable. Fire policy registers exist for the Hand-in-Hand insurance company for 1696–1865 (Ms 8674–8, 166 volumes), the Sun, 1710–1863 (Ms 11936–7, 1,262 volumes) and the Royal Exchange, 1753–9 and 1773–1883 (Ms 7252–5, 173 volumes). All are held at the LMA. If these huge numbers of registers, arranged chronologically, sounds daunting, do bear in mind that there are a number of indexes. There is an online name index for the Sun from 1800–39. When researching a book about Richmond murders last year, I was pleased to discover that in March 1834, Thomas Smethurst (who was tried for the murder of his bigamous wife in 1859) took out a policy with the Sun on his apothecary's business in south London; although he was not to qualify as an apothecary for some months later! There is also a card index at the LMA for the Sun's policies between 1714–31 (Ms 17817) and a microfiche index to both Sun and Royal Exchange policies for 1775–87 (Ms 24172). Those for that other major London insurer, The Phoenix, are located at Cambridge University Library.

Some companies were registered, and for those which were so, and dissolved from 1844 to c.1980, it is worth visiting TNA and checking BT

41 (up to 1860) and BT 31 thereafter. Although records for most businesses which ended prior to 1860 have been retained, most of those after 1860 have not (there would be too many to have kept them all), and even for those which exist, the files have often been weeded. However, the key documents, such as memoranda and articles of association, lists of shareholders, directors and managers, should exist, at least for some of the years of the company's existence. TNA also holds archives of the canal and railway companies nationalized in 1947.

If your ancestor was in business but went bankrupt, there may be a notice of bankruptcy in the national and/or local press. *The Times* online would be useful place to search, as would *The London Gazette*. The local press would probably announce this, too. Until 1869, debtors could be imprisoned; archives existing at the LMA and TNA.

Building applications, often indexed by the name of the builder, are located among council minutes and can be a valuable source of information about what work your builder ancestor carried out. Some local authority archives have indexes to workers in particular trades; Lewisham Archives have lists of local brickmakers and gas workers.

Licensed to Kill?

Many occupations required the practitioner to hold a licence from either a recognized trade body or magistrates, and this is a good way of finding out about an ancestor, if these records survive, which many do. The LMA holds licences for many men who worked in London's markets in the past. They have, for Billingsgate fish market, porters' licences from 1877–1948 and carriers' licences from 1953–62, and there are drovers' licences for the Metropolitan meat market at Smithfield from 1877–1963. There are lists of drovers' convictions from 1870–1931, too! Lists of licences to publicans exist at the LMA, arranged by year and then by parish, they list dates, licence holders and the name of the public house. They mention if anything was known to the detriment of the applicant for the licence – occasionally previous clashes with the law may be mentioned. There are also registers of applications for music and dancing licenses. Councils and their committees also list licences for stallholders in local street markets (records held at local authority record offices).

The LMA (WR/RS, MR/RS) holds licences for professions who needed the signatures of officials in order to practise their trade. This also had a religious/political dimension in some cases. To hold any civil or military office from 1673 to 1825, a man needed the signatures of churchwardens confirming he had received Holy Communion according to the Anglican rites, to show that he was not a Catholic or a Dissenter, and therefore was deemed politically reliable in the Anglican state. However, Dissenters who were willing to be flexible (Occasional Conformists) with their consciences might take communion just once a year in order to qualify for office.

As mentioned in Chapter 4, church courts granted licences to a variety of professions, including midwives, surgeons and teachers until the nineteenth century.

The City Livery Companies

In the Middle Ages, a number of livery companies were formed in the City, eventually numbering over 100, and encompassing numerous trades and professions, including leather sellers, apothecaries and booksellers, to name but three. These companies had extensive powers over the individual trades which they represented. They could fix prices, working conditions and regulate the quality of goods for sale. They could also prohibit trade by non-members and undertook the training of apprentices. Once a man became a freeman of the company he could legitimately set up shop in the City. In fact, trading in the City was prohibited unless a man was a member of one of these companies, though he did not necessarily have to be of the company in which he was trading. In order to become a freeman, a man had to either undertake several years of apprenticeship, or if his father was a member of the company (through patrimony), or rarest of all, through redemption, when a man could buy his way in. However, as the centuries passed, their role altered and became more and more involved in charitable undertakings and education; the Stationers' Company founded the Stationers' School in Hornsey in the nineteenth century for example. Most still survive to this day and are involved in such roles.

Records of freemen and apprentices exist for most of these companies, dating from the Middle Ages to the twentieth century. Those for the Grocers' Company date from 1345–1652 and 1686–1952 for membership, and for apprentices from 1457–1505 and 1629–1933, for example. Most are available at the LMA on microfilm. These records can give the name, date of birth and address of the apprentice, and perhaps his father's details, plus details of with whom he was apprenticed and for how long. For the Apothecaries' Company, for example, there are registers of the Court of Examiners, for the apprentices had to take examinations (after 1815). These tell which apothecaries the apprentices worked under, the hospitals where they worked and which subjects they were taught. It then states when they were examined and whether they passed or not. Since apprentices had to be successful in all counts, some had to retake examinations a number of times. However, some companies have not deposited their records at the LMA, such as the Leather Sellers, and anyone interested in these should contact the Clerk of the Company in the first instance.

It should be noted that the membership of these livery companies was low, and decreased as a proportion of the men in London engaged on that particular undertaking increased as time went on. If, for example, your ancestor was working as a leather seller near St Paul's Cathedral in the early eighteenth century, it is highly likely that he was a member of the company in question. However, if your ancestor was engaged in the same trade in, say, Bermondsey in the following century, it is highly unlikely that he would have been a member. The archivist to the company informed the author that he receives many enquiries from those with London ancestors involved in the leather trade who they imagine must have been members of the company, but he has to inform them that this was not the case.

Public-Sector Employment

We now turn to another major source of employment. Once local government was a very small-scale affair – Ealing council in 1863 only employed two full-time officials – but in the twentieth century and beyond, this is no longer the case. Councils each employ many hundreds of people, from rubbish collectors to grave-diggers, from architects to librarians. As ever, it is easier to learn about senior employees, as directories usually list heads of department and perhaps their assistants. Employee records as such are few and far between, but minute books may refer to new employees being taken on, and long-serving officers retiring. Senior officials, such as borough architects, should appear in minute books where decisions are recorded. In-house magazines produced by trade unions and other organizations may give useful details, such as social activities, including sports and other teams, and their members. Some council minute books, though, do record information about quite junior employees, detailing pay rises, training and other information. There may be employee record cards, as there are for all employed by Southall Council in 1955, giving personal and employment histories.

Politicians

It is relatively easy to learn about MPs from official publications (*Dod's Parliamentary Guides*) and the press, for well-known London politicians from John Wilkes in the eighteenth century to Boris Johnson in the twenty-first, but many more men and women are involved in local government. In 2010 there are seventy-three London MPs, but over 2,000 councillors in borough councils and the GLA, and given that there were once about treble the number of local authorities in London before 1965, there were even more councillors. In my career, I am frequently asked by researchers who are convinced that their ancestor was a former mayor to produce lists of mayors of all the local authorities covered by the present borough. Some researchers are quickly disillusioned to learn that their ancestor was a councillor but never mayor.

In the past councillors would be listed in directories, with the name of the ward they represented and sometimes they feature in local yearbooks/official diaries, which often give a brief summary of their education, family, career and interests as well as the committees of which they were members. Official council diaries give listings of which committees councillors served on for that year and also when council and committee meetings were held (so you could track down on which evenings your ancestor was busy at a meeting). They will also appear in council minute books, listed as attending if nothing else, for both meetings of the full council and for those committees they served on. If you discover that your ancestor was on the Finance Committee for 1906–12, you could ask to look at the committee minutes, which all local authority archives hold in great number, and read through them. Council minute books also record deaths of serving and former councillors, often including biographical and family information.

Local newspapers are another good source for the history of councillors and would-be councillors. In the lead-up to any local election, there will usually be brief biographies of each candidate, and what they stood for, as well as which party they represented. Election leaflets often give brief biographical information, including educational and family details, as well as a summary of party policy. Anything controversial about a candidate, of course, will be suppressed. James Hudson, prospective MP for Ealing North in 1945, did not state he had been a conscientious objector during the First World War. Election results will tell you how successful they were. Obituaries of local politicians are regular staples in the local press.

Civil Servants

As the seat of central government from the eleventh century, most of the government's employees have worked in London, and as the scope of governmental activities increased in the nineteenth and twentieth centuries, their number has soared. However, the survival of records concerning individual civil servants is patchy.

As ever, it is easier to find out about those who held senior grades. *The British Imperial Calendar* from 1809–1972 listed those at senior grades, with name, rank and department and educational achievements. It was produced annually and was renamed the *Civil Service Year Book* in 1973. Other, more specific publications cover particular departments, such as the *Foreign Office List* (1852–1965) and the *Colonial Office List* (1862–1966), amalgamated in 1966 as the *Diplomatic List*. Earlier civil servants can be located in *The Royal Kalendar*, 1767–1890. Incomplete series can be found at TNA.

Some service records for 1836–1976 are held at TNA, in CSC 11, but these are mostly of individuals who were particularly noteworthy or high ranking. Departmental records only exist for the Treasury's officials in series T 268; staff records of Higher Division Clerks, 1889–1919 are in T 268/1–7. There are some records for some senior officials in T 273 for the period 1945–56. There are some files on female civil servants, at T 216/428, T 215/1030–4 and T 216/713. Details of officials from 1557 to 1745 may be found in the *Calendars of Treasury Papers* and *Treasury Books*, which are published and indexed. Conscientious objectors of the First World War employed by the Inland Revenue and those who enlisted without authorization can be located in IR 81/163 and 116 respectively. Some employed in the Atomic Energy Authority are noted on card indexes (AB6/2367). All these are available at TNA. The Society of Geneaologists' Library has the Civil Service Commission: Evidences of Age, 1855–1880, which lists applicants with copies of birth and baptism certificates, and work is currently ongoing on their indexing.

The Police

Apart from the railway police, the Metropolitan Police Force was Britain's first police force, founded by Sir Robert Peel in 1829, and is the largest one in terms of personnel, budget and in renown. Originally there were but 3,000 men, who patrolled central London. In 1839 they covered the whole of what is now Greater London, a fifteen-mile radius

Policeman, c.1910.
Author's collection

from Charing Cross. The police force was divided into twenty-two divisions, each responsible for a different geographical district, and known by a capital letter. H Division was responsible for the East End, for example. Most were uniformed, but a small detective force of plain-clothes men was raised, and was reformed and expanded after the 1870s. By the early twentieth century, their numbers topped 20,000 and after 1918 there were female officers, too. It also became more mechanized and increasingly professional. At the dawn of the twenty-first century, the force is radically different, being larger, more diverse in terms of its workforce, and is under more democratic control.

The archives for its personnel are to be found at TNA, because it was originally under the control of the Home Secretary, so was part of central government's records (county forces were under the control of the county magistrates, then the county councillors and so are often held in county record offices).

There are various sources of information about members of the force.

Probably the best method is to begin by using the alphabetical list of men who joined, which covers 1830–57 and 1878–1933, which has been microfilmed (MEPO 4/333–8). This will give rank, division, dates of appointment and removal, and also the warrant number, which is a key reference for further research. It would then be useful to consult the certificates of service, which date from 1889–1909, if your man's service falls within these years. They are arranged by warrant number. They give name, date of birth, former trade, with name and address of last employer, marital status, number of children, residence, dates of promotion/demotion, reason for leaving and other information. This is to be found in MEPO 4/361–477.

Registers of leavers are another key source, and cover 1889–1947 (ref. MEPO 4/339–51). Indexed by name, they give rank, division, warrant number, dates of appointment and removal. If the ancestor might have died in service between 1829 and 1889, check MEPO 4/2, which is indexed and gives the cause of death. For those first few thousands of recruits, HO 65/26 is an alphabetical register, 1829–36. Early recruits from 1829–30 can be located in MEPO 4/31–2, arranged by warrant number. These give the officer's height and why he was dismissed (often due to drinking on duty). Attestation ledgers, 1869–1958, include signatures of recruits and their character witnesses. There are also a number of name indexes, compiled using these records, and which are available at TNA.

Last but not least, there are pension records. These were discretionary before 1890, then mandatory thereafter on the completion of twenty-five years' service. For payments to those who left between 1852–1923, there are details in MEPO 21, which include information on the man's physical description, his place and date of birth, marital status and dates of service. Next of kin and other personal details may also feature therein. Pension records after 1932 are still held by the Metropolitan Police.

Police officers can also be mentioned in the local and national press if they take part in newsworthy cases or/and arrests. There may be an article on the retirement or death of a well-known officer. Some have even written memoirs, from Chief Inspector Dew in *I Caught Crippen* (1938) to the author of *The Filth* at the beginning of the next century. How accurate these are is another question – in one memoir an officer refers to a constable as having seen the Ripper, but in fact he only heard the sound of a man running away.

The City of London Police patrolled the square mile and number about 1,000 men. They were under the control of the Corporation of

London and, despite all the police reforms of the twentieth century, are the one remaining borough police force. Archives are to be found at the LMA. Service records are arranged in boxes alphabetically by surname, but there is a closure date of seventy-five years on them. When ordering the appropriate box, the member of staff will take out the file of the man you are interested in (if his records survive). Although the bulk of the file varies considerably from man to man, there is the advantage that it is all in one place. You can learn the man's date and place of birth, details of his parents, his pre-police career and his education. Moving onto his police career, the date of appointment and his service record will be detailed, with any promotions, record of ill-health and pay. There should be the date of his leaving with a comment on his record and the reason for his departure. There may also be surviving correspondence from his previous employers and letters recommending him (or not) for further employment. I found the record of one man from Scotland, who rose to detective sergeant and had an exemplary service record, but was dismissed for adultery with a married woman (he was also married at the time). Excellent material.

Before the Metropolitan Police were introduced into outer London parishes, many had their own watch forces, and records often survive of personnel. Lewisham Archives have documents listing their special constables for 1830–2. TNA holds records of the Bow Street Runners, the force predating the Met. Horse Patrol records are in MEPO2/25; for the men of the Foot Patrol, see MEPO4/508.

London Transport

In the later nineteenth century there was a myriad of conveyances for people to travel in and around London. These included horse buses, horse trams, overground railways and from 1863, the Underground. All these were run by different companies – each stretch of Underground line was operated by a different firm, whilst the bus and tram companies were diverse indeed. At the beginning of the twentieth century, electric trams and motor buses replaced horse-drawn vehicles, but the principle remained. It was only in 1933 that the London Passenger Transport Board (renamed the London Transport Executive in 1948 and more recently, Transport for London, shortened to TfL) was created to unify these disparate systems, and this method of control has remained to this day.

Many Londoners have worked for London Transport and its successor bodies over the years, but it is easier to locate details of some

Carter Patterson Transport Company employees, 1930s. Mrs Bignell's collection

employees than others. Records about individuals are closed for seventy-five years after leaving the service. Many records were destroyed ten years after the employee left in any case. There is no one place to go to view these records and it is useful to know for which company (pre-1934) your ancestor worked and when they ceased employment.

The London Transport Museum at Covent Garden, apart from being a mecca for transport enthusiasts, also has a well-stocked library. It holds copies of transport staff magazines from 1913 onwards. These often include details of staff at the point of retirement or death, or if there is any significant news about them. Work on indexing these is ongoing. The library also has some details of war memorials which commemorate employees killed in the World Wars.

TfL Group Archives, located at 55 The Broadway, London SW17 0DD (tel. 020 7918 4142), is another major source of information. Appointments are compulsory for all those wishing to visit. They hold, among other archives, some staff records and registers. These include staff registers, mainly for drivers and conductors, for the London General Omnibus Company (LGOC), one of the largest of the pre-1934 operators, from 1899, and those for 1899–1925 have been indexed. There

Men at work at the Port of London, 1920s. Author's collection

are registers of the LCC Tram service, from 1906–34. Those from 1906–15 have been indexed. There are registers of employees injured whilst at work for the period 1928–35. There are a number of staff registers for some of the underground railway firms, dating from 1863–1966.

The LMA have a number of staff lists for those employed by various railway companies from 1863–1932, which include a list of volunteers serving during the General Strike of May 1926 and a few for apprentices in the 1920s/1930s. TNA holds staff records for some of the pre-nationalized railway companies, though these are by no means complete and tend to cover uniformed staff and drivers rather than other workers. Finally, Newham Archives holds staff registers (drivers and conductors only) for the LGOC from 1899–1913. For more information, see the information sheets at www.tfl.gov.uk.

Whilst on the topic of transport, we should mention those men who worked on the waterborne traffic along the Thames, the lightermen and watermen. Apprenticeship records have already been mentioned in Chapter 6, but their careers thereafter can be traced. The quarterage books for 1764–1923 (Ms 6819, 6404, 6402, 6401) record addresses of moorings, subscriptions paid to the company and sometimes dates of death. Complaint books (Ms 6301–5) are another source, covering grievances aired by members against their fellows, from 1802 onwards. Apparently many did so, about 20 per cent of members in all, but the books are unindexed. Sunday ferry services are recorded from 1721–1831 in Ms 6292 and give the names of men who worked on the ferries on this day, giving names and money received. Registers of boats and the names of their operators appear in Ms 6308, 6309, 6311, but are not comprehensive. Finally there are account books of pensioners from 1794–1928 in Ms 6400 and lists of payments made to pensioners in the Company almshouses at Penge from 1841–1859 in Ms 6602. All these archives are located at the LMA.

There are, however, no records for a great number of people who have worked in London; for some no records were ever created and for others any which were have been destroyed. In these instances, the only way to learn a little about what your ancestor did is to read a book about that type of employment or any histories of the company they worked for. Where archives of a particular organization exist, but where none relate to individual employees, it may still be worth seeing if there are any archives which do discuss working conditions, salaries or the work which employees were engaged in.

Chapter 9

MEDIEVAL LONDON

S ome family historians do not go back beyond the early nineteenth century, before the introduction of civil registration and the national census. More adventurous ones tend to stop at the inception of parish registers in the sixteenth century. In fact, to have reached the reign of Henry VIII is no mean feat, especially if your surname is a common one, and during your research you will probably find that your surname is a lot more common than you may have supposed. It is the Middle Ages (here taken to be those centuries from 1066 to 1538) which pose a quandary. After all, the language of the law was Latin – and not the Classical Latin that is still taught in some schools, but a bastardized version, full of abbreviations and difficult to read in any case. It might also be put forward that the Middle Ages was a time of barons and abbots, with a mass of illiterate and impoverished peasants, with the bulk of our ancestors falling in the latter category. Another difficulty is that until the fourteenth or even fifteenth century surnames were not hereditary, with some men known only by their Christian names or having their occupation or village appended to this name, so tracing ancestors is difficult. Place names are often at great variance with those from more recent times. It can also be added that the Reformation of the sixteenth century resulted in not only the dissolution of the monasteries and other religious communities, but also the destruction of their records.

But these difficulties need not be wholly impossible to overcome. Yes, Latin was the language of the law until 1733, but many documents have been transcribed, translated and sometimes indexed, often by scholars in the nineteenth century. Even when this is not the case, there is no need to be able to read, or copy entire documents, to transcribe them. The important parts from a researcher's point of view are the name/s of ancestors and the relevant information concerning them. It is worth copying this section either by hand or by photography/photocopying if these are permitted. It can then be deciphered at leisure, using various published aids and guides. Eileen Gooder's *Latin for Local Historians* is a valuable help because the examples therein are mostly of the kind of medieval documents which a family historian would probably come across.

There are other issues about dealing with Latin texts. First, many of the words, including Christian names, are often abbreviated for the convenience of the clerk. Secondly, the style of handwriting altered considerably during these centuries, as did the size of the writing. Reading such texts is an art called palaeography and taught to trainee archivists. Sir Hilary Jenkinson's and Charles Johnson's two-volume *English Court Hand, 1066–1500*, gives numerous examples of texts from the eleventh to the fifteenth century and the companion volume includes Latin transcripts, allowing you to recognize words from the plates which should help when looking at the documents you are interested in. Finally, mention should be made of Charles T Martin's *The Record Interpreter*, which includes a medieval word list with English translations, a glossary of standard abbreviations, lists of place names and Christian names and surnames. After all, if the name Ade was encountered, it might not be understood without this text that the name Adam is meant. Also remember case endings. Thus endings of Latin names vary. Most record offices should have copies of these reference works.

Another factor to bear in mind with medieval documents is that the dating is not in the style we are used to. A document will not be dated 25 October 1415, but rather on 25 October in the third (regnal) year of the reign of Henry V. Even if you know the year in which a monarch acceded to the throne, in order to accurately date such a document you need to know the exact date, and here C R Cheney's *Handbook of Dates for Students of English History* (2000) will be useful, as it sets out all the regnal years, instantly enabling a reader to find out the year of the document in which they are interested. This practice continued for the dating of deeds into well into the eighteenth century. Some documents are dated by reference to a saint's day and in pre-Reformation England there were many of these, so again a good reference work, such as the aforesaid Cheney's, is a useful tool. Dating may be by year of grace, i.e. Anno Domini, and whereas this may appear to make life easier, do remember that the English calendar before 1752 was Old Style, with the new year beginning on 25 March, thus 12 February 1516 would translate as 12 February 1517 by our standards. Some dates can be based on a bishop's year of grace or that of the pope, and in these cases, you would need to ascertain the date of their taking office.

We should also note that surnames are problematic before the fourteenth century, for a (legitimate) son might not have the same name

Brass of Henry Mylett and family, St Mary's Church, Perivale, 2010. Author's collection

as his father, and they might be known by different names throughout their lives, perhaps in relation to their trade or birthplace/address.

And we should bear in mind that many of our medieval ancestors were literate to an extent and were accustomed to the use of documents, even outside the monasteries. Many documents which have already been mentioned began to exist in the Middle Ages. These include wills and the records of livery companies. After the Norman Conquest, a complex and detailed administration emerged, far more so than had been the case in the centuries of Anglo-Saxon rule.

At the end of the Middle Ages there were about 50,000 people living in London and these people left records in their wake, albeit unevenly, and much the same can be said of succeeding centuries. Urban residents also tended to be more literate than their rural counterparts. If you plan to research your medieval ancestors it is best to work slowly backwards, beginning with your sixteenth-century ancestors. Parish registers for many London parishes date back to 1538. If you can locate your ancestors there, this is the best first step. You are now ready to step back into the Middle Ages.

Manor Court Rolls

The best records to begin with are those of the manor. They record the largest number of names and those of people of quite humble social origin, which for this period few other documents, saving the poll tax records, do. Seek the manor records for the place where your post-1538 ancestors resided. Land was held in the form of manors throughout the Middle Ages and beyond. These were economic units and could vary in size and population. The lord of the manor (usually absentee, as he would hold several manors) held part of the land, termed the demesne. Then there would be the free tenants who paid the lord a cash rent for their land, and the villeins who worked for part of the time on the lord's land. Records of individuals were often held on behalf of the lord of the manor. Manor court rolls record land transactions and administrative business (the court leet, held about once a month) and minor disputes and criminal offences (the court baron, held less often) among manorial tenants (these records continued well into the eighteenth century). Manor courts sat frequently, sometimes even monthly.

These documents are usually set out in the same way, which makes them easier to deal with once a few have been looked at. For the courts leet, at the top of the parchment roll will be the name of the type of court, the day of the week and the date. Then there will be the list of penalties paid by those tenants who did not attend the court. Those non-attendees who did not send apologies were given heavier fines (known as amercements). Then there is a list of changes in tenancy, including surrenders and admissions, and details of entry fines paid. When a tenant died, this would be noted and his heir named in what is known as an inquisition post mortem (about property, not on how the individual died). They would have their right acknowledged and would pay a forfeit, often in the shape of a beast, termed a heriot. There may also be a list of witnesses. There should also be a little information about the individual who inherited the land, with his age, and proofs given by witnesses of this fact. Other new tenants, who purchased their tenancy, would also be named here.

For courts baron, there is a list of disputes to be dealt with, with names, detail of offence and penalty paid by the offenders. There may also be a list of the court jury and officials present. Court rolls for Ruislip Manor, for example, show that in 1246, Isabella, Peter's widow, was fined 18 pence for her son John's trespassing in the lord's wood. Hugh Tree's beasts were in the lord's garden and he was fined 6 pence, whilst Walter Hill and Hugh Slipper stood as his securities. In a later court roll,

Lucy Mill committed adultery and had her property seized by the manor.

Apart from court rolls, there were less common documents. These are rentals and surveys of the manor which made from time to time, often when the manor changed hands, and these documents, as with the court rolls, often list people and describe their holdings. For urban parishes, street names are often given.

In order to track down the whereabouts of such documents, use the Manorial Documents Register, which is currently incomplete but includes Middlesex and Surrey. It can be searched online at www.nationalarchives.gov.uk/mdr/. The LMA holds the archives of many manors in Middlesex, but some are held at TNA and elsewhere; the colleges of the two ancient universities held several manors in southern England and so the library of a particular college may be a place you might have to visit; Westminster Abbey muniments room holds some.

Some manorial court rolls have been transcribed and so are more easily accessible for most researchers – some for early fifteenth-century Harrow are found with the originals at the LMA for instance. Some record societies have also transcribed some medieval court rolls.

Tax Records

Although there were no regularly imposed taxes or rates in this period, monarchs did need their subjects' money from time to time, especially to fight wars against the French and Scots. Occasional taxes, or subsidies or levies, were imposed from the thirteenth century onwards. The most well-known were the poll taxes of the early years of the reign of Richard II (1377–81) which helped lead to the Peasants' Revolt of 1381. These were taxes, usually set at a flat rate, on all adult men, with a few exceptions, such as servants. Women did not pay. There was no variation for income or wealth. Apart from creating outrage amongst many, they also resulted in lists of most of England's male population being created, organized by county. Relationships in families and occupations are sometimes given. What is even better is that these lists have been transcribed and published in three volumes (by Dr Carolyn Fenwick) so should be available at the British Library and Guildhall Library, among other places. The originals are at TNA, while some county record offices, such as Essex, have microfilm copies. We should note that returns do not exist for every village, but when they do, they list men, their wives and children above 14.

Tower of London, 1900s. Author's collection

There were other taxes levied in this period, of course, and for some of these records survive. They were known as 'Lay Subsidies'; these were not paid by the church (though clergymen owning land in their own right were liable). These were usually levied because the monarch needed money in wartime and were paid at a fraction of the individual's moveable goods. Those which survive exist at TNA and date from 1275–1525. However, for many of these levies, only total sums owed by place are noted. Yet there are names given for some of the levies in the late thirteenth and early fourteenth centuries, and also in 1524, when land was taxed at 20 per cent and moveable goods at 28 per cent and, because payment thresholds were low, most adult men were assessed and so named in these records. Because there was widespread evasion in both 1523 and 1543, there are very full lists for these years at TNA. Tax records can be found at TNA in E 179, but also at county record offices. For example, Essex Record Office holds transcripts of three lay subsidy returns for the fourteenth century and one for 1524–5. Two of these have been indexed and one has been translated.

Foreign merchants were taxed on numerous occasions in the fifteenth and early sixteenth centuries; these sums levied were known as Alien Subsidies. TNA, E 179, contains lists of tax payers, especially for 1440 and 1483–4, but there were numerous exemptions and evasions; the Irish were not liable after 1442, for instance. Taxes levied were a tax on alien householders (16d p.a.) and on non-householders (6d p.a.). Returns for Southwark have been calendared by J L Bolton, *The Alien Communities of London in the Fifteenth Century* (1998), and the same historian has also calendared the Alien Subsidy Roll for London for 1483 (E 179/242/25) and for Middlesex for 1484 (E 179/141/94–5). TNA also holds records of taxation paid by the medieval Jewish community prior to their expulsion in 1290, but no one has been able to trace a line of descent from these people.

City Records

The City of London created a variety of records which mention some of its citizens in the Middle Ages. They include letter books of the Courts of Aldermen and Common Council, dating from 1275 to 1689. These were originally registers of bonds and recognizances, but later were used as minute books for the two governing courts of the City. There are other minute books for the Common Council dating from 1416. Recognizance rolls cover 1285–1392 and 1437–97. Rolls of letters exist for 1350–70 and there are collections of deeds and charters relating to the statutes and customs of the City. There were the records of the governing bodies of the wards of the City, but only for Aldersgate do these survive for this period; their wardmote minutes begin in 1467 and their inquest presentments have 1510 as a date of commencement. If your ancestor was involved with the medieval Corporation of London, you may find a reference to him here.

There are also a sizeable number of records relating to courts in operation in the medieval City. The most complete records for any in this period is for the Court of Hustings, where there are records of Common Pleas 1272–1506, pleas of land 1273–1724, rolls of outlawries 1415–17, enrolled deeds 1252–1717 and brief calendars of cases which came before the court for 1448–84 and 1506–1723. The assize of Nuisance also has good records, with surviving court rolls from 1301 until about 1431. A few records of the medieval sheriffs' courts exist, but there are only court rolls for 1318 and 1320 and rolls of actions for 1407–98. Finally there were royal courts, such as the assize of fresh force (1442–51), assize of novel disseisin and mort d'ancestor (1340–1436), escheat rolls for the City, 1340–77, 1388–9, and rolls of pleas before the itinerant justices at the Tower, 1244–6 and 1276. Coroners' rolls exist for 1300–78, but with many gaps in this range.

Some of the City parishes also have some records dating back to the Middle Ages, but these are few in number. It is, however, worth checking the lists of what is held that predates parish registers. St Alphege London Wall has churchwardens' accounts from 1527 to 1864 (as do a few others) and several parish archives include deeds from the fourteenth century. St Stephen Walbrook even has rate assessments from 1483 to 1948. All these City records are to be found at the LMA.

Records Searchable Online

There are a number of records which can be searched without going near a record office or library. The four main categories, all from TNA, are Ancient Petitions (SC 8/2, 5–6), which cover the period from the early thirteenth century to the early seventeenth century, Early Chancery Proceedings (C 1/2, 5–6), Depositions in Exchequer lawsuits (E 134/2, 5–6) and Inquisitions post mortem, for 1415–85 and 1509–1640. The latter were accounts of the goods and lands of deceased persons, together with details of the heir (if any). Many calendars of earlier inquests have been published. If the sought name/s are found, there will be a catalogue number and then a trip to TNA is needed. You will need to check all variants of the name, because there was no standardized spelling of names in this period – Shakespeare's surname was famously spelt variously in his lifetime. There are books at TNA which list variant spellings of many names.

Deeds

Property transactions were as important in the Middle Ages as in any other time. There are a number of different types of deeds, and since they mention individuals who were transferring land, they are clearly an important potential source, but, as ever, it is those who are landed who will be recorded.

In the late nineteenth century, scholars did an incredible amount of work on transcription, translation and indexing of medieval archives. Calendars were also produced. In this context, a calendar means, not an exact copy, as with a transcription, but an abbreviated version which should include all the most important parts of the original. This means that accessibility to these records is far easier, for a researcher who will not have to spend time trying to read the handwriting of the Middle Ages (and it might be in English, too). Many of these records concern land transactions. *The London and Middlesex Feet of Fines* is an indexed record of a number of deeds, arranged chronologically. Feet of Fines refers to the bottom part of a tripartite agreement which was retained by the royal court. One excerpt reads as follows, taken from the reign of Richard II:

> Walter Kempton, clerk, Thomas Aston, John Kynbell, and John Thurston, and Thomas Gynes of Westminster, and Matilda, his wife. Premises in Westminster. Anno 9.

Other deeds can give far more extensive information. A deed of 1289 from TNA, referred to by Jenkinson and Johnson in their *English Court Hand*, tells us a lot more. It begins with the property owner granting land to another. We learn that the former was Walter de Clive, son of Roger de Clive, and that property is passing from Walter to one Roger le Cheyner, a mercer. The property is in the parish of St Anthony in the City of London and is near to that of William de Bettuna and Adam de Blakeney. There then follow various details about the property, including dimensions. At the end of the deed are the names of eleven witnesses. Even if your ancestor is not the buyer or seller, he might be mentioned therein and this document would thus tell you that he was alive at the time the deed was sealed.

There are a wide range of other deeds. Charter rolls dating from 1199–1517 are to be found at TNA. These record grants of land and privileges to organizations, but often give names of those involved and witnesses. They have been calendared for 1226–1517 and full texts have been transcribed for 1199–1216. The Royal Chancery issued Close Rolls, which are another key source, and include deeds, wills, leases, changes of name and naturalization. They are at TNA, and have been calendared from 1205–1509, with a full transcription for 1227–72. Patent rolls were also issued by the same court and include many subjects, such as grants to individuals and organizations about licences, wardship and land rights. They may also concern law and order issues. There are sixty-six large volumes of these and they cover 1216–1587. Those from 1509–47 are in the Letters Foreign and Domestic for the reign of Henry VIII. They should be available at larger libraries; such as the British Library, the Guildhall Library and TNA. Fine rolls record payments for privileges, to enter land which had been inherited, freedom from knight service, safe conducts and pardons, running from 1120 to 1649. They have been calendared up to 1509.

Finally, we should not forget that local authority archives often contain other deeds, some of which may date to the Middle Ages. These are originals and have often never been transcribed, calendared and published, so you will need to see these in the raw, as it were. They are written on parchment and, unlike nineteenth-century deeds, can be very small in size and so very concise. Some details will already be noted in the archive listing of the item; at a minimum this will be the names of the parties concerned, the land involved, the money changing hands, and the date (where known). Deeds can also exist in ecclesiastical archives as the church acquired or was bequeathed property, and also in university archives, too.

Deeds tend to be very formulaic, which makes them less difficult to deal with. Near the beginning will be the names of the parties to the deed, which might include other family members, then the transaction, concluding with the date and possibly a list of witnesses.

G R C Davies's *Medieval Cartularies* is a good introduction to the topic for those who wish to know more.

Surveys

The Domesday Book of 1086 is a record of landholding, and is the most famous work produced by the Norman administration. It notes who held which manors and often who was the previous landholder (often a deceased Saxon nobleman). There are many published transcripts of it, some of which are indexed, and copies should be available at most large libraries. Yet not all of the country was included; and from our point of view, it is worth noting that the City of London was among those parts of the country which were not. However Middlesex was, as were those other counties adjoining London, now parts of Greater London. Only the major tenants are included, so the number of names is minimal. Yet if you suspect that your ancestor might have been a major landowner in the late eleventh century, it is worth a look.

There were less known surveys of landholders, too. The Ladies Roll or Rotuli de Dominabus of 1185 was one, and this included the county of Middlesex. It listed lands held by female landholders, mostly widows and daughters of tenants in chief (i.e. those who held land directly from the monarch). Minors were also included. A printed transcript was published by the Pipe Roll Society of 1913. In the following century, a Book of Fees, which was a collection of records from 1198–1293, relating to land tenure throughout England, was created. It is arranged year by year and then by county. You can see the original at TNA (E 164/5–6), but it is easier to use the transcription, found in *The Book of Fees*, a three-volume series published by HMSO between 1920 and 1931.

Moving forward in time, there are the Hundred Rolls, though the most important for our purposes is that made in 1279–80. This lists individual landholders in each manor, but also includes the names of jurors and bailiffs, as well as their land and how much they were paying for it. Sometimes even unfree tenants are listed. As Edward I himself noted, it was meant to be 'fuller and more detailed than the survey carried out by the Conqueror'. Although not all the returns have survived, crucially, from our point of view, those for part at least of Middlesex have survived. The surviving returns are to be found in the second of the two-volume *Rotuli Hundredorum* (1818). This is in Latin, but has an index to names and places.

Church Archives

The medieval church had great power, even though the Norman monarchs curtailed its jurisdiction over criminal cases. It is hard to overestimate the importance of the church in people's lives in this period – even authoritarian monarchs (such as Henry II and his youngest son, John) had to bow to its power – and it is important to realize that there was only one church until the Reformation. Reference has already been made to the myriad courts in London which dealt with wills and whose archives are held at the LMA. Church courts had other responsibilities, too. The church still held courts to uphold public morals, punishing adulterers and so forth. It is estimated that about a tenth of the population at some time came before it. Act books, some of which have been published, list offenders brought before the courts, details of the offence and the court's verdict.

For St Paul's Cathedral, the administrative centre of the diocese of London, there are a number of medieval archives which survive. There are charters and statutes, 1099–1813, cartularies for the twelfth–fifteenth centuries, chapter act books, 1411–48. Cathedral accounts exist from 1276, dealing with repairs to the fabric, and for the bakehouse and brewery, as well as more general accounts for various senior officials. If your ancestor was a merchant in the City, a payment to him might be recorded here. Finally, there were indulgences granted to those who gave money for the rebuilding and repair of the cathedral; these date from 1201 to 1387. They are held at the LMA. The English Episcopal Acta project has resulted in the publication of two volumes of charters issued by the bishops of the diocese from 1078 to 1228. These have been transcribed in Latin, but there is a synopsis in English for each and there is a useful index to people, places and things.

Westminster Abbey has considerable archives stored in the abbey's muniments room, and some of these can be used for medieval genealogy. These include chapter books, accounts, deeds and coroner's records.

It is also worth recalling that medieval brasses in London churches might be worth examining, though not all of these survived both the Reformation of the sixteenth century and the Commonwealth of the seventeenth. For a list of brasses in London and Middlesex, see Mill Stephenson, *A List of Monumental Brasses in the British Isles*.

City Companies

As has been stated, the City livery companies began their existence in the Middle Ages and a number possess records dating back to their early history. Some of these are court minutes, such as the Armourers' and Brassiers' Company (1413–1948). Memorandum books and financial records for some companies date back to the fourteenth and fifteenth centuries. A few even have membership lists and apprenticeship records dating back to the fifteenth century, too. *The Guide to Greater London History Sources*, vol. 1, *The City of London*, should be consulted to see a very brief overview of the type of records for each company, and for the date range for each.

Contemporary Accounts of London

There are few published contemporary histories of London during the Middle Ages. One is the Anglo-Saxon Chronicles, which are several accounts by various clerics and which continued to be written until the mid-twelfth century. But it is primarily a national history, with a few references to London. In the nineteenth century, several London medieval chronicles were published in volumes of the *Camden Society* (available at the Guildhall Library and TNA). John Snowden's *Liber Albus*, published in 1419 and reprinted in English in 1862, gives an account of life in the medieval City which is certainly not without its grim side. It is indexed by places and names. In the sixteenth century, however, London was written about by John Stow. He discusses many facets of life and social history of the City of London, taking the reader on a journey through the City, street by street. Stow was writing during Elizabeth's reign, but he recounts London history, chiefly drawing on William Fitzgerald's twelfth-century Life of Beckett, as well as providing contemporary information. He mentions many people, and most editions of Stow's Survey are indexed by street and person. Even if your ancestor is not mentioned, he gives you an impression of what life was like in London at the end of the Middle Ages. Lists of other medieval accounts of London can be found in Caroline Barron's work, such as *London in the Late Middle Ages: Government and People, 1200–1500* (2005).

Miscellaneous

A few other sources should be mentioned. If your ancestor was a clergyman, you can check the published lists of graduates, as noted in Chapter 8, or if you know the parish, check the church's history or list of incumbents in the church itself. If a lawyer, some of the Inns of Court published listings begin in the fifteenth century. Remember that the PCC wills begin in the fourteenth century.

Researching your ancestors in the Middle Ages is probably the most challenging aspect in genealogy, for the reasons outlined at the beginning of this chapter. But it is not an insurmountable task, unless your ancestors were at the bottom of the social heap at this time. Provided that you can establish where your ancestors were in the sixteenth century, with luck they may have lived in or near that district in earlier decades and so the manorial court rolls can be checked. If they lived in the City of London, you are more fortunate for there are more archives surviving for the inhabitants of this part of Greater London than there are for, say, rural Middlesex, but then the City's population was greater than the latter, so this should not be surprising. You should certainly be very careful with making assumptions as to who your ancestors were, given on the whole less available evidence. It would also be useful to study some of the guides to medieval Latin, too, and see some sample texts, otherwise the sight of a court roll in microscopic writing in a dead language might prove too frightening.

Chapter 10

LONDON UNDER ATTACK

L ondon has been under attack by external enemy forces from the time of the Boudicca revolt in the first century AD to the rocket attacks of 1944–5. Londoners have rallied to the defence of their monarch, their government and their city in all cases, though we only know who they were in relatively recent times. This chapter predominantly looks at London civilians who have been caught up in conflict, whether as volunteer soldiers, civil defence workers or as casualties, but will also spend a little time on men who enrolled in the regular forces.

Pre-Twentieth Century

Although London's citizenry were involved in numerous conflicts at home and abroad from earliest times to the emergence of the Tudors, we know little of them. However, there are a number of sources which may be worth investigating for the Middle Ages. The first concerns those who came over with William the Conqueror. The best source for these is A J Camp's book, *My Ancestors Came Over with the Conqueror* (1988). Very few people, of course, can trace their ancestors this far back, and usually only through a female line. A list of some of those who fought on Henry V's side at Agincourt in 1415 can be found in *The History of the Battle of Agincourt . . . the Roll of the Men at Arms* (1827). Thousands of men who fought in the Hundred Years War (1337–1453) are listed at www.medievalsoldier.org. Finally, there was a military muster roll taken of Middlesex in about 1338. It lists, parish by parish, some at least of those able-bodied men of the county, along with their weapons, who were eligible for military service. Whether they did see active service, against either the French or the Scots, is unknown, but this list of about 1,000 names is a useful tool, especially if you had an ancestor in that parish in this period (there is more consideration given to medieval ancestors in Chapter 9). This item is located in a roll at the LMA; it is written, of course, in Latin.

There were numerous volunteer forces for London's defence from the

THE END OF THE "BABY-KILLER."

Zeppelin being hit, c.1915. Author's collection

seventeenth to the early nineteenth century. However, we know more about those who were officers than the majority of men who served in the ranks. For example, there are published lists of men who officered regiments on both sides during the Civil Wars, and these have been published in various books (C Firth and G Davies, *The Regimental*

History of Cromwell's Army (1940) and S Reid's *Officers and Regiments of the Royalist Army* (4 vols, 1985–8)). London was a centre of support for the Parliamentary cause and so most in our region will be found, if at all, in the Parliamentary army. Royalists, such as John Evelyn of Deptford, found it most prudent to not take up arms. Those on the war's losing side suffered, and there is much about them and their finances in two indexed calendars at TNA: *Calendar of the Proceedings of the Committee for Advance of Money, 1642–1656* and *Calendar of the Proceedings of the Committee for Compounding . . . 1643–1660*. Militia and volunteer forces were called into being in London from 1660 to 1745 during various crises – the Venner rising of 1661, the anti-Catholic riots of 1688, the Jacobite scares and numerous other riots – but as before, we might uncover names of officers, but never of the rank and file.

That having been said, there are a number of militia lists for the Tudor and Stuart periods. Some are held at TNA. These are lists of over 300 pikemen and musketeers of 1539. Another roll thirty years later lists 6,000 Londoners. Other rolls cover 1590–1601, giving names of hundreds of men, with details of their birthplaces and current parish. The LMA holds City muster rolls for a number of years between 1682 and 1724. There are two very useful guides to the location of militia records: J S W Gibson and A Dell, *Tudor and Stuart Muster Rolls* (1991) and J S W Gibson and M Medlycott, *Militia Rolls and Musters, 1757–1876* (1994).

Then there are the records of London's oldest military unit, if we except the Yeoman of the Guard. This is the Honourable Artillery Company, founded in 1537. Muster rolls exist from 1611 to 1862 and then onwards for officers only (the earlier rolls were lost during the Civil Wars). These give the names, ages, heights and ranks of those men who composed the Company. All men were volunteers and there are over 30,000 names on the rolls. These cannot be inspected by the public, but the Company's Archivist must be contacted with details of any individual for whom information is required. Lists, with details of men who formed the King's bodyguards, the Yeomen of the Guard, can be found at TNA.

After the 1640s, the next conflict in which large number of men were involved in military activity was the French Revolutionary and Napoleonic Wars of 1793–1815. Although there were militia units raised in the Seven Years War (1756–63), records of these men do not survive for London. At the end of that century, with heightened fears of an invasion from France, apart from the men in the army and Navy, many flocked to join militia, volunteer and yeomanry forces, as occurred more famously in 1940. It has been estimated that, at the end of 1803, there were 35,256 men in the London, Middlesex, Tower Hamlets and Westminster volunteer forces. In the following year, there were twenty-six units formed in Middlesex and twenty-three in London.

However, although there are published Militia, Yeomanry and Volunteer Lists, produced annually for this period, only the officers are listed, with rank and date enlisted. We can learn that Thomas Clutterbuck was captain of the Great Stanmore company, that Richard Andrews was his lieutenant and Francis Schrafton the ensign, and that the first two joined on 18 August 1803 and the latter on 29 October 1803. The Spelthorne Legion was a regiment with thirty-eight officers. From 1804 the lists are indexed by name and place, and are arranged in alphabetical order by county. Yet, as before, there are no names of those who served as sergeants, corporals and privates. They were clearly not viewed as being important enough to merit inclusion as named individuals.

Some other institutions hold military archives for the late eighteenth and early nineteenth centuries. The LMA holds the enormous militia ballot for Westminster of 28,000 names. Also held there are discharge papers of 4,000 men who had seen active military and naval service and so were exempt from the usual requirement to be a freeman in order to trade in the City. Some local authority archives have archives of military bodies; Bexley has militia pay lists for Bexley parish 1803–9, Chislehurst and Footscray 1803–1805 and a muster roll for Crayford for 1803 and the total number of names in these is 500. The LMA holds information about payments made to the families of men serving in the army and militia; arranged by parish, giving the name of the man, his length of service, with dates, the name of the unit, the sum paid to his family and the number of the latter, but these are not named. Thus we learn that Francis Hayward, of St Luke's parish, served with the Royal South Gloucestershires from 6 July 1803 to 17 January 1805, and his family (a wife and one child) received 4s 4d per week.

In the middle of the nineteenth century fears resurfaced about possible invasion attempts. Men enrolled into companies of rifle volunteers, wore uniforms, drilled and practised rifle fire. Social events and competitions were as important as military aspects of their role. There are enrolment books for the 36th Middlesex Rifle Volunteers for 1860–1908 and the 10th County of London Rifles for 1908–12 at TNA (refs. WO 70/1–4 and 5–6). These are arranged roughly alphabetically by surname, then chronologically on enrolment. The regimental number, letter of the company joined, date of enrolment and attestation of loyalty, name, height, age, occupation, residence, signature and remarks on leaving if applicable are all listed here. An example from the 36th Rifles was number 5424, James Batson, aged 18, a basketmaker resident at 402 Portobello Road, Kensington, who was 5 feet 5 inches tall and who resigned from the service on 30 March 1896, having enrolled on 17 May 1892. Other men left due to ill-health, were underage, were struck off or enlisted with the regular army. Other rifle companies and volunteer units were raised; there were volunteers in Sydenham, whose archives are held at Lewisham Archives. Even where no archives of individuals exist, as in Ealing, local newspaper accounts of the activities of these regiments often cover shooting competitions and note who won prizes.

The City Imperial Volunteers was a cavalry unit which was raised on a voluntary basis during the Boer War of 1899–1902. They were 3,000 men, many of whom normally worked in the City, and so were of a rather higher social standing than most soldiers. Records are held at the LMA and TNA, but advance notice is required to view the former as they are held offsite.

Likewise, tracing London men who served in the army in the nineteenth century is certainly not impossible, but it is very helpful to know the name of the regiment served in. This is because that is how the archives are organized; there is no centralized listing. A Londoner may have chosen the Middlesex Regiment or the Royal Fusiliers. Muster rolls and pension records in the WO series at TNA can give useful information about the rank and file. We can learn that William E Bignell (1853–1933) served as a private in the Middlesex Regiment in the 1870s, in India and South Africa, earning a good conduct stripe, but being unmarried did not send any money home.

Private William Edward Bignell, c.1916. Mrs Bignell's collection

Officers, as always, are easier to learn about. The *Army List*, a publication produced annually from the early nineteenth century to date, lists the officers in all units, with rank, name and date of enlistment, decorations gained and dates of previous promotions. These volumes are indexed by name. During the World Wars, these volumes were published on a monthly basis. When a man ceases to appear, it is an indication that he has died or retired.

First World War (1914–1918)

The nation was called to arms again in 1914. Millions of men volunteered for the fighting services (or were conscripted from 1916), mostly in the army. Although about 60 per cent of the soldiers' records were destroyed in the Second World War, those that survive give important information. They can be viewed on microfilm at TNA in series WO 363 and 364, in alphabetical order. They consist of enlistment papers, showing name, address, age, occupation, physical description, army unit, rank, with details of promotions, decorations and wounds if any. They can also be viewed on ancestry.co.uk. Local newspapers often listed the men who had just enlisted, with address.

Apart from these there is an online database of medals at the TNA website which can be easily searched and gives name, rank, number and unit, with medals awarded – often only the Victory Star and the British Medal, as awarded to a Kensington man, Private Percy Orlando Rush of the King's Royal Rifles. Pension records can also be seen online at TNA website. These include details of the wounds which caused a man to be so badly injured that a pension was awarded, and give a brief summary of his military career. This is useful because the soldiers' records mentioned above for the man in question do not survive. Therefore the pension details for Private John Christie (1899–1953) tell us about his brief active service in 1918 and his injuries caused by mustard gas, as well as payments made to him thereafter because of his injuries. If these records are viewed online at TNA there is no fee, otherwise a small payment is required. They can also be viewed at ancestry.co.uk.

If your ancestor died in the war, as over 124,000 Londoners did, the Commonwealth War Graves Commission website is worth checking online (www.cwgc.org/debt-of-honour.asp?menuid=14). The name of the deceased can be typed in, and his record will show name, unit, rank, date of death and burial place if known (this website can also be used for the fatalities of the Second World War and later conflicts, too). To gain more information about him, check the local newspaper for the weeks after his death. Do not expect to see anything relevant as soon as he died, as news travelled slowly and often men were thought missing before definite news of their death was known. The local newspapers usually gave details of the man's education and occupation, his family (including relatives also serving or killed) as well as his military service and any decorations, often including a quote from his commanding officer. There may also be a photograph, though as with most photographs appearing in the press at this time, they tend to reproduce badly. Names also appear on local war memorials, though not invariably. For example, the Southall War Memorial lists no names and some places raised money for an additional wing to a local hospital as a practical thanks for the lives laid down by their townsmen – rather than a monument with a list of names. Some places also commissioned rolls of honour as bound volumes, listing those killed, usually in alphabetical order, with rank, regiment and decorations, though most of these are incomplete listings. War memorial websites also exist, often put together by enthusiasts, and one exists for Lewisham memorials. Some workplaces also commissioned rolls of honour. The LCC did, listing men by department (there is also an index), who were killed and those who were not. One entry for a man in the architects' department reads thus:

Coombes, Francis John (1914–1919) MSM, mentioned in despatches; staff sergeant, RE [Royal Engineers], France 2 years 6 months, Italy 15 months.

War memorial, Northwood, c.1920s. Author's collection

3056. - SOLDIERS MEMORIAL AND GREEN LANE (Central), NORTHWOOD.

There was also a published National Roll of Honour of the Great War, in several volumes (volumes 1–3, 7 and 13 cover London), and though it is far from complete, it is a useful source and quick to check (copies are available at TNA). There are a number of volumes, each arranged alphabetically, of men who served, with brief information about their military service.

We should also remember that local newspapers gave information about local men who were awarded medals, who were wounded and/or taken prisoner, as well as those who were killed on active service. However, finding this information is less easy than locating information about fatalities, because dates of such occurrences (or even if any occurred at all) are rarely known, so this will be a speculative search. Lists were also printed of men who had enlisted, with addresses, and, from 1916, men who were called up but who had not responded to the summons were also listed, again, with addresses.

Sometimes there were lists published of local men who had enlisted. These may appear in the local press. Or they may have been published by businesses. A major department store in Southall, in 1915, published a list of men who had enlisted, arranged by unit, giving rank, decorations if any and whether they had been killed or wounded (to date). With the introduction of conscription in 1916, tribunals were formed in each borough to question men who were unwilling or unable to serve. Newspapers often covered these cases, and councils created records themselves about the outcomes of these tribunals. Some of these survive in local authority archives. One example was the son of Acton councillor and historian, William King-Baker, whose appeal was turned down and who was sent to a unit. In some cases, businessmen were given a few weeks or months to put their affairs in order before donning khaki.

Although there was no Home Guard in the First World War, special constabulary units were formed to guard places thought to be in potential danger. Information about their activity and possibly members may appear in the local press. In Hackney and Stoke Newington there were 'National Reserve' forces formed in 1912–19 and membership records exist for both at Hackney Archives.

Several hundred people were killed by zeppelins and aircraft bombing raids in 1915–18, but there is no one list of fatalities. If an ancestor was killed in such a manner, as identified from the death certificate, there may be a reference in the local press, though in wartime reporting was often guarded due to censorship. The best single source is an excellent typescript by John Hook, 'They Came, They Came', dated

1991. It details every air raid, in chronological order, and includes quotations from contemporaries, both British and German. It is also well indexed by names and places. A copy can be found on the shelves of the LMA's library and there are volumes by borough to be found in many London local authority archives. Such bombing helped lead to anti-German rioting and newspaper reports give details of those arrested for attacking German shops – often these were women and youths. Magistrates' court records at the LMA would also be useful here.

Second World War (1939–1945)

The Second World War had an even greater impact on the civilian population of London, in part because of the far greater use of aerial bombing by the German air force. The records of men serving in the armed forces are not open for public inspection. However, copies can be made available to the men themselves and their next of kin by writing to the Ministry of Defence Records Centre in Glasgow, though the intention is to move these to TNA. As with the First World War, large employers often had plaques installed in the place of work listing employees killed in the war, as did most churches. The LCC lost 1,121 members of staff during the war and, of these, over a fifth were female. War memorials sometimes listed names, though, as with the previous war, not always. As ever, these memorials are not always as complete as they should be, and sometimes names have been added to them in subsequent years.

Apart from the armed forces, many men, usually too old to join them or in reserved occupations, volunteered. In May 1940, due to fears of an imminent German invasion, the government called for volunteers for the Local Defence Volunteers, soon renamed the Home Guard and known to many as Dads' Army. Over a million men joined these units and there were many battalions of London men, usually based on geography. The Home Guard was stood down in 1944. Service details can be obtained by the next of kin by writing to the Ministry of Defence as noted above. That said, the Guildhall Library holds nominal rolls of battalions of the City and Essex Home Guard units. Home Guard activity is often referred to in the local press, though not the names of its members, and this can be useful information about what one's ancestors did in this period.

Many more people were enrolled in various of the civil defence organizations, which included war reserve constabulary, volunteer firemen, hospital staff, rescue workers, air raid wardens, ambulance drivers and so forth. There were also firewatchers, clerical and canteen staff to back up those better known roles. Many of these jobs were part-time, and it should be recalled that the Luftwaffe bombed London only by night, because there was far less risk of being shot down. So, after a hard day at the office or factory, many Londoners then had to spend one or more evening a week on call for additional and potentially hazardous duties.

Some local authorities kept detailed records of their citizens who were employed in such a manner. At best, there will be records of each individual, in alphabetical order. These will give name, address, age, ordinary occupation, civil defence role, the date they enrolled in such, details of any training courses and equipment issued, and date they ceased (possibly because of enlistment in the armed forces). Because there are no electoral registers or directories for 1940–4, this is a useful method of tracking down individuals at this time. If they were air raid wardens, it should list the post they were attached to, and other civil defence archives should state its location. On the other hand, the local authority's relevant archives may have been disposed of, leading you to be unable to ascertain much about your ancestor's wartime career, unless your ancestor has passed on information about his experiences.

Danger from the air had been anticipated by the government and nation throughout the 1930s, especially after the aerial bombing during the Spanish Civil War and from such alarmist films as *The Shape of Things to Come*. It was feared that London would be obliterated by bombing and the population either dead, wounded or panic-stricken; an estimate in 1937 was that a sixty-day bombing campaign would leave 600,000 dead. London was the worst affected city in Britain and it was certainly deadly, with the Blitz on London from September 1940 to May 1941, and the rocket attacks of July 1944–March 1945, as well as lesser attacks in other times. This resulted in over 25,000 dead and many more wounded.

Most borough councils in London kept meticulous records of property bombed within their jurisdiction. This was because some properties which were damaged needed to be destroyed, whilst others could be repaired. Owners were later compensated for their losses, and so reliable records were needed. Air raid wardens were required to record each 'incident', giving date and time, property damaged, and to what extent, and the type of bomb. However, the surviving records are certainly diverse in nature. Lewisham council created an alphabetical card index system to the properties damaged or destroyed in the borough, though the records of the adjoining borough of Deptford, which was proportionately worse hit, were less well kept. There are no

Bomb damage to High Holborn, c.1940. Author's collection

surviving council records for properties damaged in Southall, but for adjoining Ealing there is an alphabetical listing of property damaged, with date and type of bomb, as well as extensive files of air raid warden reports, in chronological order. In some cases, there are no indexes to property damaged and the records are arranged in date order, so if you do not know when or if your ancestor's house was bombed, a search could be time-consuming.

Newspaper reports of bombing are very limited, though not wholly worthless. Reports in the local newspapers were frequent, but addresses are not given. Instead you will be told, in a Hackney newspaper, for example, that houses in an eastern suburb have been damaged, and perhaps a church or school has been hit. None will be named. This is because it was feared that precise information would be used by the enemy in their future raids.

Where newspaper reports are useful is that they sometimes list fatalities. A headline in *The Acton Gazette* in late 1940 mentioned the deaths of Abraham Feldman and other family members. Using the Acton directory of 1940, we can note that the Feldman family lived in Twyford Avenue, at number 34. On the subject of civilian deaths, the Commonwealth War Graves Commission produced a great register of civilians killed. For London, this is subdivided by borough, and then arranged in alphabetical order. There are a few sentences for each individual, with full name, age, address, occupation, date of death and location of death (which could have been in hospital if not outright). It is often wise to check for other names as well as those of the same surname. In the Feldman case mentioned above, such a search revealed a non-family member at that address; perhaps a domestic servant. Most local authority archives will have the sheets of this register which pertain to the boroughs in their jurisdiction. However, they will not list those who were injured, and these far outweigh those who were killed. Hospital records may be useful here, if they survive, but as said in Chapter 7, most patient records are closed for 100 years except for next of kin. Yet there are exceptions: Lewisham Archives hold a list of those in Deptford injured in the bombing.

C Company, 16th battalion, Home Guard, Bermondsey, 1944. Mrs Bignell's collection

It should also be remembered that empty properties in London were often requisitioned by the local authority under emergency powers. Some were used to house homeless families and some were used to store furniture from bombed-out houses. Perhaps your ancestor's house was used in such a fashion? If so, the local authority may have lists of requisitioned property and further information about these; some of which were not returned to private hands for some years after the end of the war.

Children in wartime had mixed experiences. There were plans to evacuate children made prior to the declaration of war. Most of the families in the boroughs in the LCC district were encouraged to have their children evacuated at various points in the war: most famously on 3 September, but also in the summer of 1940 after the Fall of France and in the summer of 1944 with the onset of the rocket attacks. Some of the outer boroughs were also encouraged to evacuate children. However,

this was never compulsory. Only about half of the children of Londoners left the capital; often to go to the South West, Wales, East Anglia and counties to the north of London. Many came back quite soon, and by early 1940 most had done so.

Records pertaining to individuals are scarce. The county councils, who oversaw the schemes, did not keep records of who was evacuated. School log books often state how many children were evacuated, to where, and when, and which teachers were involved. But they will not state which children went and which stayed. Some schools may have created special registers of evacuees, so these will be useful. There may be information in the local press, usually showing pictures of smiling children with farm animals. These should feature both in the local press of the town to which the children had been evacuated as well as that from whence they came.

Personal letters and memoirs, as well as oral history recordings, may be useful here. The Imperial War Museum had a project to collect the latter in recent years whilst there are still people who have such memories. Some had happy times of their evacuation and made lasting friendships with those families they were billeted with. Others found it difficult to be apart from their parents and away from their familiar surroundings, and relations between evacuees and their hosts were not always happy. William Bignell (1927–2009) of Hornsey wrote to tell his parents to fetch him home, such was the misery he endured in his first billet.

Civil defence organizations persisted after 1945. Councils promoted the formation of civil defence organizations on a county scale. These were intended to provide a trained civilian volunteer corps who could assist the police and emergency services in the event of any major disaster, such as an air crash, as in Southall in 1957. It was also thought that they could assist in the aftermath of a 'limited' nuclear strike too, though the effectiveness of such was open to doubt. There may be newspaper reports of their meetings and activities; most councils kept minute books for the council's civil defence committee, and these may help with names.

There are, therefore, a number of places you can look to find whether your London ancestors were affected by conflict. They can hardly fail to have been affected by the World Wars, and information available at the local authority archive covering the district where they lived, TNA and the Ministry of Defence should be able to document much of this. It is more difficult for earlier conflicts, but again, TNA, the LMA or local authority archives may hold the information you seek.

Chapter 11

LONDON'S INCOMERS

London's death rates, as recorded in the eighteenth-century Bills of Mortality, were always higher than recorded births, yet London's population rose. This may well have been partly due to faulty recording, but was also due to a constant stream of people arriving in London, chiefly for work. Richard Whittington was not the only one who thought, at least at one time, that London's streets are paved with gold. Many of these incomers, such as the author, came from another part of England, in search of work, but many others came from across the seas. Dr Watson put it like this at the beginning of the first Sherlock Holmes novel, *A Study in Scarlet*, that London 'was that cesspool into which all the idlers and loungers of the Empire are irresistibly drained' and he included himself among this number (he had just arrived, and in ill-health, from India). We shall now look briefly at the different peoples who have arrived in England over the centuries, and for many this meant London, before discussing the available sources for tracking them down.

In the Middle Ages there were immigrants into London from a variety of places. Many went elsewhere, of course, but many stayed in the capital, too. There were Irish, Flemish and Jews in London at this time, often concentrated in certain professions, mostly offshoots of trade. They often faced hostility and sometimes even official persecution. The Jews were expelled from England in 1290. Flemish merchants were murdered by the revolting peasants in 1381 and felt the wrath of the crowd in the Evil May Day Riots of 1517. Irish workmen who offered to undertake building work in Shoreditch in 1736 at reduced wages incurred the wrath of native builders.

However some welcomed new arrivals, especially if they looked as if they would be of benefit to the state. French Huguenots, suffering from religious persecution in France in the late sixteenth and late seventeenth century, were welcomed partly on religious and ideological grounds, but also because many of them were skilled workers in the silk industry and could make financial contributions to the Exchequer. Many settled in Bethnal Green and Spitalfields. Some joined the British Army and it is estimated that in the eighteenth century, one in ten colonels was of Huguenot stock, including Jean Ligonier (1680–1770), commander in chief in the Seven Years War. Likewise with the Jews. Daniel Defoe wrote,

> The Jews have particularly fixed upon this town [Hampstead] for their country retreats, and some of them are very wealthy; they live there in good figure, and have several trades particularly depending upon them and especially, butchers of their own to supply them with provisions killed their own way; also, I am told, they have a private synagogue here.

By about 1800, there were between 15,000–20,000 London Jews.

There were also black and Asian people in London from at least the sixteenth century; often they were servants, most famously Francis Barber, Dr Johnson's servant, or sailors. There were several thousand in the eighteenth century and a small black presence remained throughout the nineteenth century.

In the late nineteenth century, the East End was where many immigrants settled, especially Jews from Eastern Europe and Russia, who were fleeing persecution. Between 1881 and 1901, about 150,000

The Rothschild mansion, 2010. Author's collection

140

people arrived in Britain. Many worked in textile industries and many lived in crowded conditions, in great poverty. Yet some Jews were very wealthy businessmen, and none more so than the Rothschild family of bankers.

After 1945, the pattern of immigration into London shifted dramatically. The best known early instance of this is the arrival of Jamaicans on the *Empire Windrush* at Tilbury Docks in 1948. Black and Asian immigration, particularly from colonies of the British Empire, was significant. Most of these were from either the Indian subcontinent or from the West Indies. But there were also immigrants from Europe; former Italian prisoners of war settled in England, as did many from Poland, some of whom had fought against the Axis powers. Motives were mixed, but economic reasons were strong for many; leaving poverty-stricken regions in the hope of a more prosperous life. Fleeing from political persecution was a reason for some, too, especially when changes of government resulted in harsh conditions. Refugees from tyrannical regimes, such as Hungarians and Czechs fleeing from Soviet aggression in 1956 and 1968 respectively, Asians from Idi Amin's Uganda in the 1970s or war-torn countries, such as Somalia in the 1990s, are more recent examples of immigrants. Finally, the opening of Europe's borders led to an influx of Polish immigrants after 2004. Most of these new arrivals came to London, partly because there were already fellow nationals there and also because London seemed to present most opportunities for work. Certain parts of London are known for particular immigrant groups, as had been the case in earlier centuries; so black people were more numerous in south London and parts of north London; Asians in the East End, and parts of northwest and outer London; Poles in west London, French in the Kensington district.

Many of the family history sources already mentioned in this book apply to immigrants, too. Census returns, for instance, disclose the country where an individual has been born, whilst directories will list heads of households and businesses. But there are a number of unique sources which should be used when researching ancestors who have arrived from overseas.

There are two websites which may be of use. The first is www.movinghere.org.uk. This covers nineteenth- and twentieth-century immigration of Jews, Irish, black and Asian people. It includes oral testimonies of immigrants, different reasons for the upheaval of arriving in a new country, the opportunity to download free photographs, newspaper reports and other pertinent material. There are research hints and the opportunity of searching TNA catalogue for more information. For black and Asian immigration prior to these centuries, try www.nationalarchives.gov.uk/pathways/blackhistory/.

Early Immigrants

Most of those arriving in Britain before the nineteenth century were from the European continent. These were French Huguenots and German Protestants who were fleeing religious tyranny from their home Catholic states. The former are well known, in part because of the work of the Huguenot Society, in publishing and indexing relevant records. *Returns of Aliens in London, 1523–1625* is a published source, giving names of foreigners in the capital and the taxes paid by them (alien was a term for a foreigner). Then there were three surveys of aliens living in London, two in 1571 and one in 1618. These can be viewed at TNA in SP 12/82 and 84 and in SP 14/102. Huguenots in London tended to settle in Spitalfields and Soho. The Huguenot Society (www.huguenotsociety. org.uk) can be contacted directly about Huguenot ancestors (for a fee), or you can see the published documents at TNA or Guildhall Libraries. Palatine (German) refugees in London can be found in TNA, T 1/119, giving names and numbers of dependants.

Other sources include the indexes to the Calendars to State Papers Domestic (1509–1704) at TNA, and also the Calendars to Treasury Papers; again available at TNA and the British Library. Passes for incoming people in the eighteenth century were issued by the Secretaries of State, and noted in the SP 44/386–411 for 1697–1784 and FO 366/544 for 1748–94. There are some indexes to these; in the forementioned State Papers calendars, up to 1704, then in the Calendar of Home Office Papers, 1760–75. The political turmoil caused by the French Revolution in 1789 led to a new surge of refugees from France, this time escaping political, not religious terror. Some returns to the Aliens' Office for 1810–11 survive at FO 83/21–2. Newcomers, from 1793 to 1836, were subject to the Aliens Act of the former year, but very few records survive. Newcomers had to register with the Justices of the Peace, giving name, address, rank and occupation. This information was sent in the form of certificates to the Home Office. After 1826, such records are found in HO 2, and are indexed up to 1849 in HO 5/25–32. There is an index at TNA for the names of Poles and Germans who arrived in 1847–52. No certificates survive after 1852.

Class HO 3 contains lists of alien passengers made by masters of ships arriving at English ports, from 1836–69, with a gap for 1861–6. They are arranged chronologically and there were four lists per year. They give name, profession and country of origin, name of ship travelled in and port of arrival. In 1843, nearly 8,000 arrived in London; which was over one half the total number of these immigrants. Alien arrivals for 1810–11 and 1826–69 can be searched online by name at ancestry.co.uk.

The LMA has a few records relating to the registration of aliens for the late eighteenth century. There are accounts for aliens in Middlesex, completed and signed for a number of northern Middlesex parishes for 1797, and returns made by overseers or householders for a few other parishes in Middlesex and Westminster. These aliens include French, Italians and Germans. One example is of a house in the parish of St Anne's, where it was noted, 'Charles Chevalier de Beaumont, alien, has taken the house no. 43 Gerrard Street . . . on the 5th of October, 1797'. Living with him were four named lodgers, all French, and 'belonging to the opera house'. These are listed under MR/A for Middlesex and WR/A for Westminster.

There were relief efforts directed to Spanish and Polish refugees in the later nineteenth century. For the Spanish, TNA, PMG 53/1–9 cover payments for 1855–1909 when the last one died. For the Polish, PMG 53/2–8 covers allowances given in 1860–99 and T 50/81–97 for the years 1841–56.

Naturalization

Many immigrants became legally British subjects by either receiving letters of denization or, in later centuries, by being naturalized. This meant that they had all the privileges of natural-born Britons, which included voting rights. Letters of denizen exist from the sixteenth century, when about 7,000 were granted. A number of volumes of the Huguenot Society volumes cover the centuries prior to 1800. These are volume 8, *Letters of Denization and Acts of Naturalisation for Aliens in England, 1509–1603*, volume 18, for 1603–1700 and volume 27, covering 1701–1800. The latter two volumes also cover Ireland.

Later naturalization records are located at TNA. These include naturalization papers, 1789–1871 at HO 1 and are indexed. Home Secretary's certificates, 1800–1980 (from 1962 indexed annually) are indexed in HO 409/1–11. Correspondence about naturalization has been indexed thus, for 1841–78 at HO 45, 1879–1934 at HO 144, and can be searched for online. HO 405, covering 1934–48, can be searched for by surname, but after that date, the correspondence files are closed for general access, though a FOI request could be made (you can do this online). Indexes to naturalizations give name, country of origin, date of certificate and place of residence. Successful application certificates for 1844–73 are at C 54 and those from 1870–1987 are in HO 334.

Certificates of naturalization give name, address, occupation, place and date of birth, nationality, marital status, name of spouse, names and nationalities of parents.

Notices of application for naturalization also appeared in the local press for the district in which the immigrant resided. *The Acton Gazette*, for instance, noted these in its pages in the 1950s and 1960s and these are indexed in the index volumes for this newspaper, by name. The address of the applicant is also noted.

Remember that most immigrants chose not to go to the expense, time and trouble of being naturalized. The decision to do so often depended on wealth. I recall an instance of an excited genealogist telling me he had a photocopy of the naturalization papers, full of information, about his great-grandfather. I had to tell him that, although the two men shared the same name, everything else did not match the known facts about him, so sadly it was unlikely that this record concerned his ancestor.

Passenger Lists

Records of ships' passenger lists from countries outside Europe can be another useful source. These are to be found at TNA, BT 26 and cover 1878–88 and 1890–1960. They are arranged chronologically and state the name, age, marital status, occupation and destination address of the arrival, with port of origin and port of arrival and name of ship. From 1960 this system of recording was discontinued. They are available on ancestry.co.uk and can be searched by name. However, there are no lists of those arriving by aeroplane in the twentieth century, nor are there for those who arrived by the boat trains from French or other European ports. Departure lists are to be found in BT 27 for 1890–1960. Both sets of archives have been digitalized and can be searched by name on TNA website, free at TNA, otherwise a fee is payable.

One example, from BT26 is Beresford Brown. The record states that he was born in Kingston, Jamaica, in 1909. He took a French ship, the *Colombie*, arriving in Plymouth on 29 December 1950, and was noted as being a musician. He did not have an address in England.

Passport registers exist from 1795 to 1948, giving number, date of issue and name. Before the 1920s, the destination of the journey was also stated. These passports were not books, but sheets of paper issued just for one journey. Records are located at TNA.

Internment

During the World Wars, natives of those countries opposed to Great Britain (Germany and Austria for both wars, plus Italy during the Second World War) were suspected of being sympathetic towards the enemy. Therefore, many were interned. Alexandra Palace in north London became an internment camp during the First World War; the Isle of Wight during the Second. There are some partial lists for these periods at TNA. WO 900/45–6 for the First World War and HO 214/5 for the Second. MEPO files also cover internment during the First World War, and there are various lists; one is organized by county and by borough, and lists names and addresses of enemy aliens. These are far from comprehensive however. MEPO 2/1796 lists those London Germans who were interned, had their property sequestered and now applied for it to be returned. Older internees can be found at HO45. Appeals against internment are noted in TNA files HO 382 and 405.

About 8,000 Germans were interned during the Second World War amid new security concerns, but very few personal records survive; about seventy-five are to be found in TNA, HO 214. Some were deported to ports outside Europe, and lists are in TNA, BT 27. There are also those in TNA, HO 396, 307, sets of Germans, Austrians and Italians and spouses who were either interned or considered for the same between 1939 and 1947. Dates of birth, address, occupation and details of employers are listed here.

Aliens had to register with the local police, but few archives survive. From 1884 to 1989, about 1,000 registration cards for the Metropolitan Police areas exist (MEPO 35, available on microfilm at TNA). Most cover the 1930s, so if you have Jewish ancestors who arrived at that time, this source may be useful. They include name, date of birth and date of arrival, employment history, marital status, details of children and naturalization. Most of these cards were destroyed after ten years, and those surviving represent less than 1 per cent of those created. They are closed for 100 years after the subject's birth, though a freedom of information (FOI) request could be made.

The 1905 Aliens Act meant that aliens could be deported if they had become paupers or criminals. Registers of deportees can be found at TNA, HO 372 for 1906–63. The records list name, nationality, offence, date of conviction and whether the deportation order was revoked or not. These records are arranged in date order. Some criminals and prostitutes evaded being deported by entering into a marriage of convenience with a British subject and thus becoming naturalized.

Newspapers and Publications

Some immigrant communities have and had their own newspapers, which specialize in providing news about their own members. The oldest is *The Jewish Chronicle*, which began in 1841 and copies since then are available at the London School of Jewish Studies as well as at the British Library Newspaper Library at Colindale. These have obituaries and marriage announcements and so are an important source for family history. A century later, the *Dziennik Polski* was established in 1940 and still exists to this day as a daily paper, but at time of writing will soon be weekly. More recently there is *The Nation*, founded in 1981, aimed at black Britons, and *The Eastern Eye*, aimed at those of Asian descent, founded in 1990. These are tabloid newspapers, but may well be a useful source of recent information.

Immigrant communities have also promoted their leading citizens in yearbooks. There is *The Jewish Year Book*, *The Indian Who's Who in Britain* (from 1979) and in 2000, there were books of British black achievers and a similar volume for Asian high flyers. Each of the latter two listed 1,000 people in various fields, financial, business, the media, sports, politics and fashion, with a brief biography of each and pictures. As always, it is easier to find out about someone if they are prosperous than if otherwise. All of these published works are national; but the majority of these achievers have London connections, even though some may no longer live there.

Oral History

For recent social history, oral history is a major tool, though the method itself is not new (Tudor historians were well versed in recording what elderly men told them). It is a way of imparting stories which might otherwise have been lost and have often never been written down, usually these recordings are by elderly people, though by no means all. The London Museum of Jewish Life has about 400 tape-recorded memories, the Museum of London has recordings of people from many different countries who have settled in London, and Gunnersbury Park Museum has recordings of people from South Asia and Poland, to name but three museums with relevant collections. Many have been transcribed onto paper and some translated. However, as with any other source, oral history must be dealt with cautiously as people's memories can often be at fault.

Military Records

Many Indian, Polish, Jewish and black servicemen fought alongside British and other Allied troops in the two World Wars. The British Jewry Book of Honour lists 60,000 Jews fighting in the British forces in the First World War. Some did so as part of units which were specific to their race. For example, there was the Jewish Brigade, the Palestine Brigade and the Jewish Legion. The old India Office Library collections at the British Library might hold material useful about Indians who were involved with the armies of the East India Company and later, the British Raj.

Jewish Sources

Apart from all the sources outlined above there are some which specifically relate to Britain's Jews. At the end of the nineteenth century, so great was the influx of often poverty-stricken Jews into London's East End, that the Poor Jews' Temporary Shelter was established at Leman Street in Whitechapel. Each ship carrying Jews which arrived in London was met and adult men were greeted by a representative of the shelter. The records of these men who accepted shelter and help between 1895 and 1914 have been entered into a database (http://chrysalis.itsuct. ac.za/shelter/ shelter.htm) and as there are over 43,000 names therein, it is well worth a look. A similar institution was the soup kitchen for the Jewish poor, founded in Spitalfields in 1854, and whose archives are located at the LMA.

There were two London schools which catered for Jewish children. The most important was the Jews' Free School. The admission and discharge registers for the school, showing details of pupils, can be downloaded from the 'Moving Here' website hosted by TNA website. The Westminster Jews' Free School has deposited its records at the LMA.

Other records are held in a number of local authority archives. Marriage notice books for Stepney from 1926 and from Bethnal Green from 1837–78 and 1920–65 exist at the Tower Hamlets Local History Archives. The Norwood-Ravensworth Archives in Stanmore hold records for the Jews' Hospital and Orphanage, Norwood, which existed from 1795 until 1963. This institution first housed ten boys and eight girls, but numbers grew and in 1860 there were 140 inmates. A fee is payable per hour's searching. Camden Local Studies and Archives Centre holds registers for Highgate Cemetery.

Those with Jewish roots should check www.jgsgb.org.uk and

www.jewishgen.org. Most seventeenth-century Jewish immigrants were wealthy merchants from southern European countries. In the following century they mostly came from central and eastern Europe.

Asian and Black Immigrants

Those people arriving from the British colonies could do so without any restrictions or any need for naturalization until the Immigration Act of 1962. Those travelling from the Commonwealth from 1948 (which by this time included India) could apply for registration as UK citizens, and applications to do so from 1948 to 1987 are to be found in TNA, HO 334. These list name, name at birth if different, address, date of birth, marital status, father's name, and place of birth and whether he was still living. However, records after 1980 are less detailed, including only name, name at birth if different, address and place and date of birth. These are not indexed, but do have registration numbers by which they are organized; you will need to apply to the Home Office, Immigration Section, for these.

Many black people were recruited into London Transport, to the NHS as nurses in particular and to various branches of the catering trade, as well as to industry. In many cases, prospective employers went to the West Indies and elsewhere in order to recruit. Material at the TfL archives and in hospital archives (see Chapter 8) should be useful here. However, there are a few earlier miscellaneous records. These include those of the Committee for the Relief of Poor Blacks, 1786–7 (TNA, T 1/631–8, 641–7). This was for those black people who wished to be sent to Sierra Leone, and there are lists of intended settlers and those receiving relief. For the twentieth century there are, after 1962, labour vouchers, which had to be granted by the Ministry of Labour in order for someone to gain entry into Britain. A sample of surviving vouchers can be found in TNA, LAB 42, for 1962–72, and in LAB 48 for 1973–5. Many black men in the nineteenth century were sailors, so documents at TNA concerning seamen, BT 98–9, should be consulted for surviving crew lists for the years after 1800, though only a 10 per cent sample survive. Commonwealth citizens could also be deported after 1962, and relevant recommendations and actual cases for 1962–3 only can be found in TNA, HO 372/29 and HO 344/73.

Polish Immigrants

After 1945, about 200,000 Poles settled in Britain. This was the largest single group of European immigrants. Many had fought alongside

Britain in the war and felt unable to return to their homeland, which was now under Communist rule. They formed the Polish Resettlement Corps, part of the British army, from 1946 until demobilization in 1949. Some records exist of these men at TNA, WO 315/8 (army lists and nominal rolls) and WO 315/13–14 relate to medical staff. There was also a Committee for the Education of Poles, which existed until 1954, and some files exist for successful students (TNA, ED 128/42–75). We should also note that many Poles were naturalized between 1940 and 1948 (TNA, HO 405). Requests for military records for Poles who served with British forces during the Second World War should be addressed to APC Polish Enquiries, Building 59, RAF Northolt, West End Farm, Ruislip, Middlesex HA4 6NG. Another useful address is the Sikorksi

Katyn Memorial, Gunnersbury Cemetery, 2010. Author's collection

Centre and Polish Institute, 20 Prince's Gate, London SW7 1PT (tel. 020 7589 9249). They hold the archives of the Polish Government in Exile (to 1990) and the papers of senior Polish officers and politicians. They also hold a list of Poles in London in 1923, though this is far from complete, and details of consular staff and those who came into contact with them. Remember that most Poles are Catholic and so their children attended Catholic schools and churches in London, so their records may be useful. Ealing's Polish Catholic church specifically caters for the borough's Poles.

Irish

Although immigration from Ireland was the largest single source of immigration into Britain until the 1970s, there is relatively little trace of their arrival. This is because, apart from brief periods, such as the Second World War (when Ireland was neutral), there have been no restrictions on the Irish moving to Britain and so no records were created especially for them. There are some references in TNA, HO files to political gatherings of Irishmen in London in the nineteenth century. Registration papers for those becoming British citizens (1948–69) are to be found in HO334. There may be records of Irish social clubs in London, such as that of the Gary Owen Club in Hammersmith in the 1940s, or, as with the Poles, for Catholic churches and schools.

General Sources

Remember that immigrants will appear in many of the sources already listed in this book, such as electoral registers, directories, telephone listings, military records, criminal records, the census and parish registers. However, apart from their names, there may be little to state that they are newcomers. Some may have taken anglicized names, and a few have the term 'Blackamoor' appended to their names, as some black people did in sixteenth and seventeenth parish registers. Archives of places of religion may also be useful; almost always these are still held at the institution itself and so application for access should be made there.

Sources Overseas

If your ancestors came from overseas, you will need to travel back to their and your roots in order to discover the fullest information about them. If your ancestors were from the West Indies, you'll need to visit the record offices and libraries there, but it is recommended that you read the various research guides available in the UK first in order to learn what information you might find and where it is located. As always, contact the repository you want to visit in advance and order material prior to visiting in order to make the best use of precious and limited research time. If your ancestors were from central or eastern Europe, the devastation of the Second World War may have resulted in the loss of many archives. However, though it used to be said that the destruction of archives in the Irish Civil War meant that research in Ireland was very difficult, there are still plenty of archives there which do survive and can be accessed.

This chapter has tried to cover the major sources for the history of people arriving in London over the centuries. Much is held at TNA, and much has been made available online. These should provide useful starting points for your research.

Chapter 12

HOUSE HISTORY

Now that you have found out about your family's history, or need a break from it, why not find out about where they lived? House history is nowhere near as well known as family history; there are few programmes on television about it, not many books about it nor any magazines nor societies of people who are interested in the topic. Yet house history is easier than family history because the sources are finite and not subject to restrictions which can apply to sources about people. This chapter looks at the key sources for the history of London's houses; however, I will be focusing on those built in the nineteenth and twentieth centuries, for almost all of those currently standing were built then. It will try to provide the means to answer questions such as the age of the house, who built it, when it changed hands, how it changed over the years, what was there before it existed, if anything drastic happened in its history, and what the district was like in the past. This will also give another insight into your ancestors' lives, as well as that of their abode.

Local Government Records

Before a house can be built, land must be acquired and permission to build sought. Most houses are built by a building company, who will purchase the land and then approach the local authority with their plans, detailing what they plan to build (and it will usually be a number of houses), with what and at what cost. These will then be examined, along with those of other builders at the council's Works Committee meeting. Among the committee will be the public surveyor/engineer/architect. His professional verdict will guide the councillors' decision whether to grant the builders permission, whether any amendments are needed or whether to reject the plans. Charles Jones, Ealing's borough surveyor, insisted on all houses being of a certain rateable value. Once permission was granted, the work of the council's officials are not at an end. First, the public health officials must arrange for the new houses to be connected to the borough's sewerage system, and secondly, the officials of the building inspector's department must monitor and record the progress of the building in order to check the builders comply with statutory requirements and the council's by-laws.

All this activity leaves archives which can be found chiefly in local record offices. First of all, committee meetings will list the builders and the names of the plans of the properties (these rarely survive) they submitted, with the date of the meeting, those attending and what their decision was. Yet minute books are not always indexed, so you need an approximate date of building, and then to work back from there. Drainage plans can then be sought. These do not always exist, but if they do, the local authority record office may not possess them. They may still be held by the council's planning office, possibly microfilmed, so that office will have to be contacted to ascertain if they exist and how access can be gained (for central London, drainage applications to the Metropolitan Board of Works are located at the LMA). There may be floor plans of the houses to which drainage was connected, or there may only be sketch outlines of property.

There may also be building inspection books, used by the council's building inspectors to record the progress of each building. These are arranged chronologically, but are often indexed by street. They list, for each property; the name of the builder, street name and house number, date at which various parts of the property were checked as being in order – such as the foundations, drainage, and so forth. These books also record significant changes to the property, such as extensions, building a garage or a greenhouse, along with the builders' names and dates as above.

For properties in central London, the archives of the Metropolitan Building Office should be consulted. They had to monitor construction of new houses according to the 1844 Building Act. To enforce this, district surveyors inspected new and altered buildings and made monthly reports. These returns survive for 1845–52 and 1871–1939. They are arranged as submitted, in date order, and list date of construction, address, owner, builder and builder's address. Records after 1870 give the height and number of storeys. There are also Building Act case files, covering 1855–1986 (about 40 per cent survive), and these include correspondence of architects/builders/owners about new streets and new buildings, with drawings and plans. All these archives are held at the LMA.

It will be noted that there has been no mention of an architect. Many people are convinced that, because architects are people who design houses, the house that they are interested in must have been designed

Belmont Hill, Lee, 1996. Author's collection

by one. Whilst sometimes this may be true, in the huge majority of cases, it is not. Most houses are built by builders working from a plan. Architects are expensive and are hired to design significant structures, such as major public buildings.

Although many houses are privately built, we should spare a thought for council housing. Local authorities were empowered in 1890 to construct housing for the working classes, though few did so, and even then only in moderate numbers, until after 1918. It was then that the government began to award councils subsidies for building council houses and this continued for decades, though there was a trend after 1945 to build tower block flats to replace slum housing in poorer parts of the capital. In 1980, 'Right to Buy' legislation offered council tenants the opportunity to buy their home, at a discount, and many chose to do so.

If the property is or was a council house or flat, there will be far more information available in the archives of local authorities. The minute books of the Public Housing Committee will include the decision-making process which led up to the construction of the housing estate, the expenditure involved, the building contractors appointed, and so forth. There may also exist plans, specifications and articles of agreement between the council and the contractors, which will give information about the materials used, how the houses were envisaged, how long construction took, among other information. When property is demolished, such as a number of tower blocks in recent years, there should be references to such decisions in the housing minute books, too.

Deeds

Since the Middle Ages, deeds have been drawn up to legally convey property from one party to another. With the increase of the middle class, deeds reached their peak in the nineteenth century, with many being created and kept. However, owing to changes in the law of property in the twentieth century, it is no longer necessary to retain deeds going back more than twenty-five years before the present owner acquires the property. Banks and solicitors have no need to retain vast numbers of deeds. This has resulted in a great many collections of deeds finding their way into local authority record offices, often via the agency of the British Records Association, which acts as a clearing house for the distribution of archives.

These deeds can cover decades of a house's history from the moment the builder or developer buys the plot of land, through changes of ownership, and increasing prices. A deed can be a very lengthy document, if it was drawn up from the mid-eighteenth century to the mid-nineteenth (usually these are made from parchment), before being reduced to a more manageable size as the nineteenth century progressed. For nineteenth- and twentieth-century deeds, the date is given in the form recognizable to modern readers and the text is in English. The text in the twentieth century is often typed.

Deeds begin with the names, addresses and occupations of those selling the property, then the same information for the buyers (or tenants). There then may be a recital of previous deeds, listing previous owners, before stating the current price/rent, and then listing what the property consists of, such as the grounds and any outbuildings. For late nineteenth-century deeds onward, there may be a block plan of the property, which also shows adjacent properties and other features, such as roads. Any restrictions on the property will be noted – for instance, not using the property as a commercial premises. Finally there will usually be the signatures of witnesses to the deed.

Many deed collections are, as stated, held at local authority record offices. They are usually well catalogued, which is a skill archivists are taught in some detail on their training courses. But the number of deeds originally created was so vast that the thousands of deeds in record offices represent only a fraction of these, and a researcher may not be fortunate enough to locate what they are looking for. As with any archives, a search on the access to archives database is worth trying. Recently the author looked for any deeds on an obscure back street in Notting Hill (now demolished) and found that there was one at the LMA.

Yet for those researching the history of London's houses from 1709 to 1938 (Middlesex only from 1889), there is another resource, which has already been mentioned in this book, in Chapter 2. This is the Middlesex Registry of Deeds, located at the LMA. This is a huge collection, not of deeds, but of a summary of each one (there are some complete transcripts for some of the later ones). It is indexed by year by the name of the seller, not the street. In order to find the seller, you could try the Valuation Books (sometimes known as the 1910 Doomsday Books) to locate the owner in 1910, and then work forward using electoral registers/rate books/directories until reaching the point when that owner is no longer resident (or look for their will, which should tell you to whom the property passed), which may well be when the house was sold. Thus, armed with the year of sale and the seller, you can then check the indexes to the deeds registry (on microfilm) to uncover the reference numbers for the actual summary of the deed. Another method of locating the owner is to ascertain the builder/developer by checking the council committee minute book, which should give their name when the request for permission to build was given. Because the builder will be the first seller, and you have a year of building, the year of sale should be shortly afterwards, and so the indexes to the deeds registry can be searched. Once the correct deed summary has been found, you will have the name of the new owner and then can work forward.

The Land Registry is another important source (www.landreg.gov. uk). Established in 1862, it covered that part of London excluded from Middlesex in 1899; before that year, registration was occasional because it was not compulsory. For a small fee, a copy of the registration records for a house can be obtained. These include details of sales, the current owner, current mortgage details, plans showing boundaries. Although there is rarely much historical information, it is always worth asking for.

If you are researching your own house, you could also ask your mortgage provider to show you the deeds and provide copies (a fee will usually be charged).

Printed Records (Other than Newspapers)

Once a property has been built, it must then be sold. Publicity leaflets are often produced when a new housing estate is finished. These will show a picture of a particular house (and all in the same development are usually fairly similar), a block plan, a list of rooms, with dimensions, building materials, the price, a map and reasons why these particular properties are so valuable. These could include proximity to local amenities, transport facilities, places offering education, leisure and employment. Some of these leaflets survive in local authority record offices among ephemera or pamphlet collections.

The builders of the Ingram Way development at Greenford in the 1930s produced a brochure which included pictures of the houses built along with the following sales pitch:

Ingram Way estate, Greenford, has a particular appeal to the thoughtful man or woman who wants the best possible value for money. This is not a haphazard built up area but a real quality proposition. You can go a long way, and study many houses quoted at higher and lower purchase prices, but you will be unlikely to find a more attractive bargain.

The site's advantages are listed; 'extremely healthy', 'well served by the GWR', 'reasonably priced at £750'. It then lists the house's internal amenities, hot water, lavatory basin, enclosed bath, indoor and outdoor toilets, points for electricity and gas and so on.

There also might be auctioneers' catalogues, which will list properties, giving reserve prices, and perhaps other details. They will also give the date of the auction, which is a valuable clue to the date of it changing hands. Again, these catalogues often survive in local authority record offices. Sometimes whole archives of estate agents exist, and these include large numbers of sales particulars and catalogues for a particular district over a period of time.

For council property, there are additional types of records. These include brochures created by the council on completion of a housing project, extolling the virtues of the properties, stating the builder, the architect (often the council's own engineer), and the materials used in construction. Then there may be tenants' handbooks, which tell the tenant what their duties are and how they can best make use of local amenities. This can often seem quite patronizing to a modern reader, but they were clearly designed to be helpful.

Newspapers

Newspapers have been regularly published in London since 1666. Since the eighteenth century they have included adverts and many of these are for property. However, few newspapers have been systematically indexed, except for those which have been digitalized and so can be searched by keyword. This does include a number of national titles, most notably *The Times*, and a number of nineteenth-century titles as mentioned in Chapter 3. Houses are usually advertised in the local press, though little is to be lost by making speculative searches in these online newspapers. I recall once making a search on *The Times* online for Ealing Village, a high-class development from the 1930s and finding an advert there, with an illustration too.

Once again, if you have a rough idea of when the house was built, you can then go to the relevant local newspaper which will be located at the local authority record office covering that district, and make a search through the property section, which, from the later nineteenth century onwards, is likely to be significant and in the same place in each issue. There may be a line drawing of a house on that development, because a number of houses are being sold, not just one. There will be the builder's name, the estate agent's name, the price of the house, a list of its features and the advantages of the location. For subsequent sales, a smaller advert will probably be placed in the local press; again, you will need an approximate idea of when it changed hands.

Houses to let are also advertised, as with this example from *The Acton Gazette* of 29 January 1904:

> Charming house to let; three years' agreement; rent £40 per annum, fitted with bath (hot and cold), electric bells etc., eight rooms, near railway and electric tram; garden front and back, 10 Cumberland Road, Acton. Apply to R. Hunt, No.2 Cumberland, Road, Acton.

There might be other references to the house and street if anything significant occurred there, but these are even more difficult to locate unless a date is known. If the house was demolished, perhaps as a result of slum clearance, as occurred to Ruston Close, Notting Hill, in late 1970, or was one of the tower blocks destroyed in more recent decades, there might be a newspaper feature; perhaps a picture.

Major municipal housing projects might also feature in the local press, perhaps with the mayor officially opening them, or shown with the first tenant, extolling the virtues of the new dwellings. Sometimes journalists might highlight scandalous housing conditions, and articles could include interviews with inhabitants. Again, a rough date is required to be able to find these, unless a researcher is ready to wade through many, many newspapers and quite possibly with no tangible result.

Some local authority archives hold collections of news cuttings on various topics, including housing, and these are easier to leaf through than microfilmed newspapers.

Directories, Electoral Registers, Rate Books and Census Returns

One of the most important details to ascertain at the beginning of your research is roughly, at least, when the house was built. This can be done by using those resources already mentioned in Chapters 2 and 5 of this book. In this case, you are using them to work backwards, not looking for a family or individual, but at an address, until you can find it no longer. So, if a property is listed in the directory for 1890, but not for 1889, then the deduction can be made that the property was built in about 1889, because, as said, the information in the directory has been derived from what was correct in the year before the year which it ostensibly covers (the same is true for electoral registers, too). However, it is worth just going back through another couple of directories, because it is possible that a property stood vacant for a time or that information about the occupant/s was unavailable.

Remember that these books were designed to record people, not buildings. Also remember that streets are often renamed and renumbered. In the nineteenth century, roads were subdivided into terraces, rows, cottages, each of which was numbered separately. By the twentieth century, councils wanted to impose greater uniformity on streets, so had most of these subdivisions abolished, with the streets were given a single name and simply numbered. Also note that many houses were given names by their owners. For example, Dr Nicholl's house in Church Road, Hanwell, was named by him Cherington House – after his birthplace. These house names were not static; new owners could give their house a new name. In the twentieth century, many of these houses were given numbers and the names disappeared. In order to circumvent these issues, it will be necessary to work back through sources year by year, rather than trying to speed the process up by leaping backward fifty or so years.

These sources will also tell you who lived in the property in question, and the 1911 census will list the number of rooms there, and whether the house was subdivided for multiple residency (very common in working-class districts until well after 1945) or whether servants resided there (very common in middle-class districts before 1939). Most important you should have a rough date of when the house was built. You can then move onto other documents.

You may also find that a notable individual once lived in the same property, which surely must rank as equivalent to finding that you are like Boris Johnson and are related to royalty. Some houses in London have a plaque on them to announce this fact to passersby, but many are not so honoured by these plaques, often because the current owners are not desirous of such publicity.

Street and House Naming

A common query among those interested in house history is why the house or, more commonly, street received its name. The process whereby a new street acquires a name is straightforward enough. The builders give a selection of names to the council and the latter choose one. It must be a name which causes no one to be offended and more importantly, must not be a name which is duplicated elsewhere in the council's jurisdiction, in order to avoid the two addresses being confused. That said, in 1954, Kensington Council renamed Rillington Place (named after a village in Yorkshire) Ruston Close, opposite Ruston Mews. Sometimes the council may approach local societies for ideas for street names, or even the borough archivist, on occasion.

Street names may reflect interests of the builders – perhaps the birthplace of the builder or that of a family member. Often streets built at the same time or by the same builder are themed; anything from Conservative politicians to famous generals, types of apple tree or towns in Australia. Names of poets are common for a cluster of street names. Sometimes a street name might reflect an aspect of local history, a notable individual, perhaps, or a large house or other feature which used to stand nearby. Streets can be named after current structures, perhaps a local pub or a transport feature. They may also be named after a contemporary event or figure.

Sometimes local authority archives hold booklets about street names, which may provide the reason why a street was named so. Otherwise, you may need to consult an old map of the district, or consult a list of former local notables. Streets can be renamed, often because of an evil association – there was a road in Hammersmith (Rose Gardens) which featured in accounts of a particularly shocking murder in 1879, so was renamed Cardoss Street. A road in Hanwell was renamed Framfield Gardens in 1907, because, as the council minutes noted, it had acquired a reputation as being associated with drunken Irishmen and so property there was difficult to sell or let. House names in the nineteenth century were usually at the whim of the owner. They may reflect a personal aspect of their life, such as where they were born.

Maps

Maps show what a district was like in the past, and so are a valuable source for house history. They will also show what was on the site of a house before construction. There are no detailed maps as we know them of London which predate the late seventeenth century. The Rocque maps of the 1740s cover central London and most of greater London, and though they show and name individual streets, the level of detail is not high compared to later maps. Even so, they do enable a viewer to have an idea of what a district looked like in the pre-photographic age. For some parishes, there are parish maps of the eighteenth and early nineteenth century, too. These often label the residences of the socially prominent (as ever, family/house history is easier if your ancestors are wealthy). Tithe maps of the 1830s–1840s have far more detail and show every property; the accompanying schedules list land usage, acreage, occupier and owner.

From 1865 onwards, and published every twenty to thirty years, are the Ordnance Survey maps. These are the most detailed and the most comprehensive survey maps available, and should not be confused with the OS maps used by walkers (the Landranger series). Those for 1865–1935 are 25 inches to the mile; thereafter, the scale is 50 inches to the mile. They show every property, together with other geographical features. Some buildings are named, usually public buildings and prominent private houses. Copies for many for the years 1865–1935 can be purchased, in a convenient size which can be folded and carried about when on a field trip, from the Alan Godfrey Map Company (www.alangodfreymaps.co.uk). Contemporary OS maps can be purchased as digital copies from the OS. Maps also show what was on

Manor House, Ruislip, 2010. Author's collection

the site of the house prior to construction. Many houses were built on what was farmland, or it could have been a former brickfield, or the former grounds of a mansion, sold off as building plots.

For central London of the 1890s, the Charles Booth 'poverty maps' are a useful source. They show how wealthy a particular street's inhabitants were, identified by colour coding – black indicating semi-criminal, gold representing the very rich. The maps can be seen online.

There are also the GOAD plans from 1967 to date. These show high streets and shopping centres and are published annually, thus giving very regular updates and allowing easy comparisons. Many councils had Second World War bomb damage maps showing where bombs fell in their jurisdiction, and the type of bomb which fell.

All these maps should be available to view at local authority record offices. They can be copied unless they are still in copyright (within fifty years of publication), and then only a portion can be copied. The LMA and TNA also have extensive collections of tithe maps and bomb damage maps.

Valuation Office Records

In 1910, a new form of property tax was introduced, in order that property owners would pay a proportion of the increases in the value of their property due to public works nearby, such as roads, lighting or drainage. This resulted in a nationwide survey of property. The tax was abolished in 1920, but if the house in question existed in the second decade of the twentieth century, these records are worth investigating. There are three types. First there are the valuation maps, located at TNA, IR121, for London. These show each property and each has a unique number marked on it. This will enable you to use the most important set of records, the Field Books, held at TNA, IR58. These list addresses, property owner, with type of ownership (freehold or leasehold), the tenants, if any, with type of tenancy, rent and its duration. There may be additional information, such as its age, the number of rooms in the house, a description, its condition, and there may also be plans and sketches. However, these are not complete. Finally there are the valuation books, usually held at the appropriate local authority record office, though a few are held at TNA. These list addresses, with owner and occupier, and sometimes give rateable values. These books are sometimes termed 'Doomsday Books'.

Pictures and Photographs

Maps are a very useful way of illustrating the district where your house was/is located. Paintings and prints of prominent streets, churches and buildings exist for most places in and around London from the seventeenth to the early nineteenth century. However, it is unlikely there will be an image of your house amongst these. Photography in London dates from 1839, and by the end of the century was very common. The postcard industry is, for the first forty years of the twentieth century, the major source for pictures of London. Many companies took advantage of the new medium and mass-produced postcards of many scenes of streets, parks, public buildings, churches, bridges and statues. Many also feature people and transport. There were pictures of transport, military, police, sporting groups and even of accidents and disasters. Most were black and white or sepia, some are tinted or hand-coloured. The coverage was uneven; with more postcards of middle-class districts than working-class ones, and more pictures of prominent thoroughfares than back streets.

These pictures can be viewed at local authority record offices. Most sell copies of some of them. You can also buy originals at postcard fairs (there is a monthly one in Bloomsbury – for details see the internet or events listings in antiques magazines) or online at ebay.

Local authority record offices also hold other pictures which are of equal interest. These could have been shot at the bequest of the local authority, perhaps when recording an important civic event, or the destruction of slum housing. Local newspapers often deposit photographs taken in the past at these places, and they also receive donations from the public. Most of these pictures are of topographical interest, so are worth investigating. Provided the pictures are not to be reproduced, most can be copied digitally or by other means. The LMA also has a sizeable collection of topographical photographs of London, as does the National Monument Record, whilst the Guildhall Library's collection of prints is impressive and can be viewed online.

Disasters

These are always good news for newspapers and also for house historians, though not of course for contemporary residents. Fire and bomb damage are deadly for houses, and though for the former one naturally thinks, concerning London, of the Great Fire, there have been numerous smaller conflagrations. House fires are recorded in the local press, and also in fire brigade archives occurrence books, which list the premises which firemen visit to extinguish fires, and the date. These books can often be found in local authority record offices.

Bomb damage during the Second World War was heavy and has already been referred to in Chapter 10. It is fairly straightforward to ascertain whether a property was damaged or destroyed by bombing, when, the type of bomb used, casualties and other information. Records of requisitioning in this period are another useful source. Some empty properties in London were taken over by the local authority and used either to house the homeless or store furniture from bombed-out buildings. These records show who owned the house, and their address, name/s of previous tenant/s and rent paid, for how long the house was in public ownership and the amount of compensation paid. There will be details of what the building was used for, too. Such records, where they survive, should be located in the record office of the local authority concerned. As ever, their survival rate is variable.

Insurance registers have already been mentioned in Chapter 8, but they can be used in house history to determine when an insurance policy was taken out, often shortly after building, a brief description of building materials used, changes in ownership over time. As said in the previous chapters, most registers of insurance companies are held at the LMA.

Inventories have already been mentioned in Chapter 6. These were common from the sixteenth to the eighteenth centuries and were appended to wills. The executors chose two or three men to survey the goods found in each room in the house for valuation purposes. This results in a list of rooms in the house, as well as the furniture within it. However, if there was nothing in a room, it would not be mentioned, and remember that only a minority of people made wills. These are held at the LMA as diocesan record office.

Books

Reading general local history books about the district where the house was located is useful for background information, because there may be accounts of particular localities, as well as pictures. If the property is in central London, there is an extremely useful series of books titled *Survey of London*. This forty-one-volume series published from 1902 to 1984 covers the inner London boroughs, is indexed and the sources used therein are referenced. Maps and illustrations also feature throughout. They detail when landed estates were sold to builders and when housing estates were erected. Pevsner's *Buildings of England* series covers London in several volumes and is useful for brief details of buildings deemed of architectural merit, often giving dates of construction and the names of architects/builders. For the social backgrounds of districts, the volumes of the *New Survey of London Life and Labour* published in the 1930s are useful, especially for their discussion of poverty and affluence in that decade.

Summary

Learning about the history of the house/s that your ancestors lived in adds another dimension to your knowledge of their lives, as well as that of the house. As with people, it will be easier to learn about some houses than it is for others. The two major sources will be held at the local authority record office covering the district in which the house is situated and the LMA, particularly for central London. Finally, it might be worth asking the current occupiers for any known information – those who have lived there for a long time should be particularly knowledgeable.

CONCLUSION

F amily history is akin to a jigsaw puzzle. You are given a few pieces at the beginning, and, with the help of those, it is up to you to find and fit the other pieces together. Each piece is important in itself, but is also a clue to other pieces, and they in turn to others. If you come to a dead end, try another piece. However, it is only you who canl decide how and when the jigsaw will end. Researching ancestors in London is perhaps more complex than elsewhere, not because there is not enough information available, but because there is so much and it can be widely scattered. London is not a homogeneous entity. It is a jigsaw in its own right, held together by various pieces of administrative and ecclesiastical tape.

Hopefully this book will have served its purpose if it has pointed readers into new paths for research. Despite the extraordinary steps that have made information available in an easily searchable electronic format, there is still much delving required among manuscripts and other traditional sources, too. This book has insufficient space to detail everything a reader may wish to know, and so the books mentioned in the Bibliography should be consulted for detailed and specific information on topics of interest. Happy hunting!

BIBLIOGRAPHY

T here are many public and private institutions in London which hold material relevant to London family history and make it accessible to researchers. Many of these, however, are national institutions, such as the National Scout Archives, so, although they contain information about former Londoners, they also have a much wider coverage. These, with a few exceptions, will be excluded from this Bibliography. Instead I will concentrate on places – archives, libraries and some museums – which contain, primarily, matter which pertains to London ancestors. Please note that, although this information was correct at time of writing, change in the archival world as with the wider world, is constant. I have refrained from giving opening hours as they are also changeable; check websites and always contact places in advance.

Please note that, before visiting any of these places, it is worth reading through their websites to learn what they have and then contacting them to ensure that they have what you want and that it is available for you to consult. Most places hold some of their stock offsite, so turning up 'on spec' could lead to disappointment and a wasted visit. All these places are free to visit, and most are easily accessible via public transport. Some have parking nearby. Some require proof of identity (official documents with signature, address and photograph) before a reader's card is granted. Check before your visit if these are needed. Generally only TNA, the LMA and the CROs demand these. Usually pencils only are allowed for the taking of notes, though laptops can often be used, as may digital photography. As always, check in advance.

London-Wide Institutions

The London Metropolitan Archives
40 Northampton Road, London EC1R 0HB (Tel. 020 7332 3820)
Email: ask.lma@cityoflondon.gov.uk
Website: www.cityoflondon.gov.uk/lma

Guildhall Library
A principal reference library for the Corporation of London, it holds the best collection of directories in London as well as an excellent library of books on London history.
Aldermanbury, London, EC2P 2EJ (Tel. 020 7332 1868)
Email: guildhall.library@cityoflondon.gov.uk
Website: www.@cityoflondon.gov.uk

Huguenot Society of Great Britain
The library and archives of the society, founded in 1885, contain much information about the Huguenots in Britain.
University College Library, Gower Street, London WC1E 6BT (Tel. 020 7679 5199)
Email: library@huguenotsociety.org.uk
Website: www.ucl.ac.uk/library/huguenot.htm

Salvation Army

Founded in East London in 1865, this organization has assisted many people in tracing lost relations through its confidential service.
101 Newington Causeway, London SE1 6BN (Tel. 0845 6340101)
Website: www.salvationarmy.org.uk

The National Archives

Ruskin Avenue, Kew, Surrey TW9 4DU (Tel. 020 8876 3444)
Email: enquiry@tna.gov.uk
Website: www.nationalarchives.gov.uk/

The Society of Genealogists' Library

The Society was founded in 1911 and its library holds a large number of transcripts, microfilm and books covering UK genealogy. There are many biographies, family trees and indexes. They also hold lectures on a very regular basis on many aspects of family history. It is open to the public for a daily fee, but if you are planning to use it regularly it would be less expensive to become a member.
14 Charterhouse Buildings, Goswell Road, London EC1M 7BA (Tel. 020 7251 8799)
Email: librarian@sog.org.uk
Website: www.sog.org.uk

Lambeth Palace Library

A major source of Anglican records (not parish registers) in London, housed in the archbishop of Canterbury's residence.
London SE1 7JU (Tel. 020 7898 1400)
Email: lpl.staff@c-of-e.org.uk
Website: www.lambethpalacelibrary.org

Transport for London Group Archives

Holds material concerning staff of transport companies which later merged to form London Transport.
55 The Broadway, London SW17 0DD (Tel. 020 7918 4142)
Email: grouparchives@tfl.gov.uk
Website: http://www.tfl.gov.uk/foi/889.aspx

Principal Registry of the Family Division

Houses wills and their indexes for 1858 onwards.
First Avenue House, 42–49 High Holborn, London WC1V 6NP (Tel. 020 7947 6000)
Email: ade.ojo@hmcourts-service.gsi.gov.uk
Website: www.courtservice.gov.uk

Army Records Centre

Not in London; but holds records of soldiers discharged after 1921, including Home Guard and National Servicemen (many of them from London).
Ministry of Defence, Historical Disclosure, Mail Point 400, Kentigern House, 65 Brown

Street, Glasgow, G2 8EX (Tel. 0141 224 3030)
Website: www.mod.uk

Barnardo's After Care Dept

Founded in Stepney in 1867 by Dr Barnardo, the organization founded and ran children's homes throughout the UK until the late twentieth century. The records can be searched for a fee.

Barnardo's, Tanner Lane, Barkingside, Essex, IG6 1QG (Tel. 020 8550 8822)
Website: www.barnardos.org.uk/whatwedo/aftercare

County Record Offices

CROs hold the archives of the county Quarter Sessions, including order books, indictments and gaol delivery books, Poor Law and hospitals, parishes and Nonconformist chapels, directories and electoral registers and much more. Many parts of London were previously parts of these counties.

Essex Record Office

Wharf Road, Chelmsford CM2 6YT (Tel. 01245 244644)
Email: ero.enquiry@essexcc.gov.uk
Website: www.essexcc.gov.uk/ero

Hertfordshire Record Office

County Hall, Peg's Lane, Hertford SG13 8EJ (Tel. no. 0300 1234049)
Email: hertsdirect@hertscc.gov.uk
Website: www.hertsdirect.org/hals

Centre for Kentish Studies

County Hall, Maidstone ME14 1XX (Tel. 01622 694363)
Email: archives@kent.gov.uk
Website: www.kent.gov.uk/e&l/artslib/archives/hme.html

Surrey History Centre

130 Goldsworth Road, Woking, Surrey GU21 6ND (Tel. 01483 518737)
Email: shs@surreycc.gov.uk
Website: www.shs.surreycc.gov.uk

Local Authority Archives

In the following lists, county refers to the pre-1965 jurisdictions (in 1965 all became part of Greater London); in some cases two counties are given. This is where, in 1889, some parishes became part of London. The authorities noted after the slash are those which were the immediate predecessors to the London boroughs they now comprise.

Barking and Dagenham Local Studies Centre

Valence House Museum, Beacontree Avenue, Dagenham, Essex, RM8 3HT (Tel. 020 8270 6896)

Email: localstudies@lbbd.gov.uk

Website: www.barking-dagenham.gov.uk/4–heritage/local-history/local-study-centre.html

Former county/local authorities: Essex/Barking and Dagenham

Parishes and places: Barking, Chadwell Heath, Dagenham

Barnet Archives and Local Studies Centre

80 Daws Lane, Mill Hill, London NW7 4SL (Tel. 020 8959 6657)

Email: library.archives@barnet.gov.uk

Website: www.barnet.gov.uk/localstudies

Former county/local authorities: Middlesex and Hertfordshire/Finchley and Hendon, Barnet, East Barnet and Friern Barnet

Parishes and places: Burnt Oak, Child's Hill, Chipping Barnet, East Barnet, Edgware, Finchley, Friern Barnet, Golders Green, Hendon, Mill Hill, Monken Hadley, Temple Fortune, Totteridge, Whetstone, Woodside Park

Bexley Local Studies and Archives Centre

Central Library, Townley Road, Bexleyheath, Kent DA6 7HJ (Tel. 020 8836 7369)

Email: archives@bexley.gov.uk

Website: www.bexley.gov.uk/index.aspx?articleid=2563

Former county/local authorities: Kent/Bexley and Erith, Crayford, Chiselhurst and Sidcup (part)

Parishes and places: Bexley, Crayford, East Wickham, Erith, Foots Cray, North Cray, Sidcup, Welling

Brent Archives

Willesden Green Library, 95 High Road, Willesden, London NW10 2SF (Tel. 020 8937 3541)

Email: archive@brent.gov.uk

Website: www.brent.gov.uk/archives

Former county/local authorities: Middlesex/Willesden and Wembley

Parishes and places: Alperton, Brondesbury, Cricklewood, Harlesden, Kensal Green, Kensal Rise, Neasden, Northwick Park, Oxgate, Queensbury (part), Stonebridge, Wembley, Willesden

Bromley Local Studies Library

Central Library, High Street, Bromley, BR1 1EX (Tel. 020 8461 7170)

Email: localstudies.library@bromley.gov.uk

Website: www.bromley.gov.uk

Former county/local authorities: Kent/Bromley and Beckenham, Penge, Orpington, Chislehurst (part)

Parishes and places: Anerley, Beckenham, Biggin Hill, Bromley, Chelsfield, Chislehurst, Cudham, Downe, Farnborough, Green Street Green, Hayes, Mottingham, Orpington, Penge, St Paul Cray, Upper Norwood (part), West Wickham

Camden Local Studies and Archives Centre

Holborn Library, 32–38 Theobald's Road, London WC1X 8PA (Tel. 020 7974 6342)

Email: local.studies@camden.gov.uk

Website: www.camden.gov.uk/localstudies

Former county/local authorities: Middlesex-London/Hampstead, Holborn and St. Pancras

Parishes and places: Belsize Park, Bloomsbury, Cantlowes, Dartmouth Park (part), Gospel Oak, Hampstead, Highgate (part), Holborn, Saffron Hill, Somers Town, West Hampstead

Croydon Local Studies Library

Croydon Central Library, Croydon Clocktower, Katharine Street, Croydon CR9 1ET (Tel. 020 8760 5400 ext. 1112)

Email: localstudies@croydon.gov.uk

Website: www.croydon.gov.uk

Former county/local authorities: Surrey/Croydon, Coulsdon and Purley

Parishes and places: Addington, Addiscombe, Coulsdon, Croydon, Purley, South Norwood, Upper Norwood (part), Sanderstead, Shirley, Woodside

Ealing Local History Centre

Ealing Central Library, 103 Ealing Broadway Centre, London W5 5JY (Tel. 020 8825 8194)

Email: localhistory@ealing.gov.uk

Website: www.ealing.gov.uk/Service/Leisure/Libraries/local-history-centre/

Former county/local authorities: Middlesex/Acton, Ealing, Southall

Parishes and places: Acton, Ealing, Greenford, Hanwell, Northolt, Perivale, Southall, West Twyford

Enfield Local Studies

1st Floor, Thomas Hardy House, 39 London Road, Enfield, Middlesex, EN2 6DS (Tel. 020 8379 2724)

Email: local.history@enfield.gov.uk

Website: www.enfield.gov.uk/

Former county/local authorities: Middlesex/Edmonton, Enfield and Southgate

Parishes and places: Bowes, Brimsdown, Bush Hill Park, Cockfosters, Edmonton, Enfield, Fords Green, Forty Hill, Hadley Wood, Oakwood, Palmers Green, Pauls House, Southgate, Winchmore Hill

Greenwich Heritage Centre

Artillery Square, Royal Arsenal, London SE18 4DX (Tel. 020 8854 2452)

Email: info@greenwich.heritage.org

Website: www.greenwich.gov.uk

Former county/local authorities: Kent-London/Greenwich, Woolwich

Parishes and places: Blackheath (part), Charlton, Deptford (part), Eltham, Greenwich, Plumstead, Woolwich

Hackney Archives Department

43 De Beauvoir Road, London N1 5SQ (Tel. 020 7241 2886)

Email: archives@hackney.gov.uk

Website: www.hackney.gov.uk

Former County/local authorities: Middlesex-London/Hackney, Shoreditch, Stoke Newington

Parishes and places: Dalston, De Beauvoir Town, Hackney, Hackney Wick, Haggerston, Hoxton, Kingsland, Lower Clapton, Moorfields (part), Shacklewell, Shoreditch, Stamford Hill (part), Stoke Newington, South Hornsey (part), Upper Clapton

Hammersmith and Fulham Archives and Local History Centre

The Lila Huset, 191 Talgarth Road, London W6 8BJ (Tel. 020 8741 5159)

Email: archives@lbhf.gov.uk

Website: www.lbhf.gov.uk

Former county/local authorities: Middlesex/Fulham and Hammersmith

Parishes and places: Brook Green, Fulham, Hammersmith, Parsons Green, Shepherds Bush, Walham Green, West Kensington

Haringey Museum and Archive Service

Bruce Castle Museum, Lordship Lane, London N17 8NU (Tel. 020 8808 4118)

Email: museum.services@Haringey.gov.uk

Website: www.haringey.gov.uk/leisure/brucecastlemuseum.mu

Former county/local authorities: Middlesex/Tottenham, Hornsey, Wood Green

Parishes and places: Brownswood Park, Crouch End, Harringay, Hornsey, Muswell Hill, Noel Park, Page Green, Stroud Green, Tottenham, Wood Green

Haringey Local Studies Collection, Bruce Castle, 1997. Author's collection

Harrow Local History Collection
Civic Centre Library, Box 4, Civic Centre, Station Road, Harrow HA1 2UU (Tel. 020 8424 1056)
Email: localhistory.library@harrow.gov.uk
Website: www.harrow.gov.uk/ccm/navigation/leisure-and-culture/libraries/
Former county/local authorities: Middlesex/Harrow
Parishes and places: Belmont, Canons Park, Greenhill, Harrow, Harrow Weald, Hatch End, Hooking Green, Pinner, Queensway (part), Roxbourne, Roxeth, Stanmore, Sudbury, Wealdstone, Woodhall, Woodridings

Havering Local History Collection
Central Reference Library, St Edward's Way, Romford RM1 3AR (Tel. 01708 432394)
Email: Simon.Donoghue@havering.gov.uk
Website: www.havering.gov.uk/index.aspx?articleid=3427
Former county/local authorities: Essex/Romford, Hornchurch
Parishes and places: Collier Row, Cranham, Harold Wood, Havering-atte-Bower, Hornchurch, Noak Hill, Rainham, Romford, Upminster, Wennington

Hillingdon Local Studies Archives and Museum Service
Central Library, 14–15 High Street, Uxbridge, Middlesex UB8 1HD (Tel. 01895 250702)
Email: archives@hillingdon.gov.uk
Website: www.hillingdon.gov.uk/libraries
Former county/local authorities: Middlesex/Hayes and Harlington, Ruislip-Northwood, Yiewsley and West Drayton, Uxbridge
Parishes and places: Colham Green, Cowley, Dawley, Eastcote, Harefield, Ickenham, Harlington, Harmondsworth, Hayes, Hillingdon, Northwood, Ruislip, Uxbridge, West Drayton, Yeading, Yiewsley

Hounslow Library
24 Treaty Centre, High Street Hounslow, Middlesex TW3 1ES (Tel. 0845 456 2800)
Email: localstudies-hct@laing.com
Website: www.hounslow.info/localstuidies
Chiswick Library, Dukes Avenue, Chiswick, London W4 2AB (Tel. 020 8994 1008)
Former county/local authorities: Middlesex/Hounslow, Heston and Isleworth, Feltham, Brentford and Chiswick
Parishes and places: Brentford, Chiswick, Cranford, East Bedfont, Feltham, Hanworth, Heston, Isleworth, Hounslow, Osterley, Pates, Spring Grove, Strand on the Green, Sutton, Sutton Court

Islington Local History Centre
Finsbury Library, 245 St John Street, London EC1V 4NB (Tel. 020 7527 7988)
Email: localhistory@islington.gov.uk
Website: www.islington.gov.uk
Former County/local authorities: Middlesex-London/Islington, Finsbury
Parishes and places: Clerkenwell, Dartmouth Park (part), Finsbury, Highbury, Holloway, Islington, Moorfields (part), Pentonville, Tollington Park

Kensington and Chelsea Local Studies

Central Library, Hornton Street, London W8 7RX (Tel. 020 7361 3038)

Email: CentralLocalEnquiries@rbkc.co.uk

Website: www.rbkc.gov.uk/

Former county/local authorities: Middlesex-London/Kensington, Chelsea

Parishes and places: Brompton, Chelsea, Earls Court, Kensal Town, Kensington, Notting Dale, Notting Hill

Kingston Local History Centre

North Kingston Centre, Room 46, Richmond Road, Kingston upon Thames, KT2 5PE (Tel. 020 8547 6738)

Email: local.history@rbk.kingston.gov.uk

Website: www.kingston.gov.uk/museum

Former county/local authorities: Surrey/Kingston, Maldon and Coombe, Surbiton

Parishes and places: Chessington, Coombe, Ham, Hook, Kingston, Malden, Norbiton, Surbiton, Tolworth, Worcester Park

Lambeth Archives Department

Minet Library, 52 Knatchbull Road, London SE5 9QY (Tel. 020 7926 6076)

Email: archives@lambeth.gov.uk

Website: www.lambeth.gov.uk/Services/LeisureCulture/LocalHistory/ Archives.htm

Former county/local authorities: Surrey-London/Lambeth, Streatham and Clapham

Parishes and places: Brixton, Clapham, Gipsy Hill (part), Herne Hill, Kennington, Norwood (part), Stockwell, Streatham, Tulse Hill, Vauxhall

Lewisham Local Studies and Archives

Lewisham Central Library, 199/201 Lewisham High Street, London SE13 6LG (Tel. 020 8297 0682)

Email: local.studies@lewisham.gov.uk

Website: www.lewisham.gov.uk

Former county/local authorities: Kent-London/Deptford, Lewisham

Parishes and places: Blackheath (part), Catford, Deptford (part), Forest Hill, Grove Park, Hither Green, Lee, Lewisham, New Cross, Sydenham

Merton Local Studies Centre

Morden Library, Merton Civic Centre, London Road, Morden, Surrey SM4 5DX (Tel. 020 8545 3239)

Email: local.studies@merton.gov.uk

Website: www.merton.gov.uk/libraries/localstudies.asp

Former county/local authorities: Surrey

Parishes and places: Colliers Wood, Merton, Mitcham, Morden, Pollards Hill, Raynes Park, West Barnes, Wimbledon

Newham Archives and Local Studies Library

Stratford Library, 3 The Grove, London, E15 1EL (Tel. 020 8430 6881)

Email: archiveslocalstudies@newham.gov.uk

Website: www.newham.gov.uk
Former County/local authorities: Essex and Kent/East Ham, West Ham, Barking (part), Woolwich (part)
Parishes and places: Beckton, Canning Town, Custom House, East Ham, Forest Gate, Hallsville, Little Ilford, Manor Park, Maryland, Plaistow, Plashet, Silvertown, Stratford, Tidal Basin, Upton, Upton Park, West Ham

Redbridge Local History Room

Central Library, Clements Road, Ilford, Essex, IG1 1EA (Tel. 020 8708 2417)
Email: local.studies:@redbridge.gov.uk
Website: www.redbridge.gov.uk/learning/localstudies.cfm
Former county/local authorities: Essex/Ilford, Wanstead, Woodford
Parishes and places: Barkingside, Ilford, Wanstead, Woodford

Richmond upon Thames Local Studies

Old Town Hall, Whittaker Avenue, Richmond, Surrey, TW9 1TP (Tel. 020 8332 6820)
Email: locstudies@richmond.gov.uk
Website: www.richmond.gov.uk/depts/opps/eal/leisure/libraries/history
Former county/local authorities: Surrey and Middlesex/Richmond, Barnes, Twickenham
Parishes and places: Barnes, Fulwell, Hampton, Kew, Mortlake, Petersham, Richmond, Teddington, Twickenham, Whitton

Southwark Local History Library

John Hardy Library, 211 Borough High Street, London SE1 1JA (Tel. 020 7525 0232)
Email: local.history.library@southwark.gov.uk
Website: www.southwark.gov.uk
Former county/ local authorities: Surrey-London/Bermondsey, Camberwell, Southwark
Parishes and places: Bermondsey, Camberwell, Christchurch, Dulwich, Gipsy Hill (part), Newington, Peckham, Rotherhithe, Southwark

Sutton Local Studies

Central Library, St. Nicholas Way, Sutton, Surrey, SM1 1EA (Tel. 020 8770 4747)
Email: local.studies@sutton.gov.uk
Website: www.sutton.gov.uk
Former county/local authorities: Surrey/Beddington and Wallington, Sutton and Cheam, Carshalton
Parishes and places: Beddington, Belmont, Carshalton, Cheam, Cuddington, Hackbridge, Sutton, Wallington, Woodmansterne

Tower Hamlets Local History Library and Archives

Bancroft Library, 277 Bancroft Road, London E1 4DQ (Tel. 020 7364 1290)
Email: localhistory@towerhamlets.gov.uk
Website: www.towerhamlets.gov.uk
Former county/local authorities: Middlesex-London/Bethnal Green, Polar, Stepney
Parishes and places: Bethnal Green, Blackwall, Bow, Bromley St. Leonard, Cubitt Town,

Isle of Dogs, Millwall, Norton Folgate, Old Artillery Ground, Old Ford, Old Tower Without, Poplar, Ratcliff, Shadwell, Smithfield, Spitalfields, Stepney, Stratford Bow, Wapping, Wellclose, Whitechapel

Waltham Forest Archives and Local Studies Library

Vestry House Museum, Vestry Road, Waltham, London E17 9NH (Tel. 020 8509 1917)
Email: vestry.house@walthamforest.gov.uk
Website: www.lbwf.gov.uk/index/leisure/local-history.htm
Former county/local authorities: Essex/Chingford, Leyton and Walthamstow
Parish and places: Chingford, Highams Park, Leyton, Leytonstone, Walthamstow

Wandsworth Libraries local History Collection

Battersea Library, 265 Lavender Hill, London SW11 1JB (Tel. 020 8871 7753)
Email: localhistory@wandsworth.gov.uk
Website: www.wandsworth.gov.uk
Former county/local authorities: Surrey-London/Battersea, Wandsworth
Parishes and places: Balham, Battersea, Putney, Roehampton, Wandsworth

City of Westminster Archives Centre

10 St Ann's Street, London SW1P 2DE (Tel. 020 7641 5180)
Email: archives@westminster.gov.uk
Website: www.westminster.gov.uk/archives/index/cfm
Former counties/local authorities: Middlesex-London/Paddington, St. Marylebone, Westminster
Parishes and places: Bayswater, Belgravia, Covent Garden, Knightsbridge, Lisson Grove, Little Venice, Maida Hill, Maida Vale, Marylebone, Mayfair, Neat Houses, Paddington, Pimlico, Queen's Park, Soho, Westbourne Park, Westminster

Museums

London has countless museums of all shapes and sizes, but two of the largest and best known are as follows. Many London boroughs also have their own museums of collections of artefacts of local archaeology and social life. Remember that most exhibits are not on view, but can be seen by prior arrangement. Remember too, that many hold archives and collections of books and illustrations, which, again, can be viewed by an appointment made in advance of a visit.

Museum of London

The museum for all aspects of London's history from earliest times to the present, with significant archaeological collections.
London Wall, London EC2Y 5HN (Tel. 0870 4443852)
Email: info@museumoflondon.org.uk
Website: www.museumoflondon.or.uk

Imperial War Museum

Founded in 1917 to commemorate the sacrifices made in the First World War; also covers the Second World War. Includes a major library and archive collections relating to these

struggles, though not servicemen's records.
Lambeth Road, London SE1 6HZ (Tel. 020 7416 5320)
Email: mail@iwm.org.uk
Website: www.iwm.org.uk

Family History Societies in and around London

Researching your family tree can be a lonely process; family members are interested in results, but may not be interested in how progress is made, colleagues and friends may not be fascinated by it, and certainly those employed in archives and libraries should not be bored with it. The best thing to do is to contact the appropriate family history society which covers the district/s your ancestors lived in, and to join them. These societies hold regular meetings, often with speakers who are expert on a particular topic that is relevant to the family history of the district that society covers. Family history societies also produce regular newsletters and their members often have special knowledge and information which may be of use to you. Try going to one. You have nothing to lose, and might find new friends and new avenues of research.

East of London Family History Society
Website: www.eoflfhs.org.uk
Covers districts in the modern London boroughs of Barking and Dagenham, Hackney, Havering, Newham, Redbridge and Tower Hamlets

West Middlesex Family History Society
Website: www.west.middlesex-fhs.org.uk
Covers London boroughs of Ealing (part), Hammersmith and Fulham, Hounslow, Kensington and Chelsea.

Hillingdon Family History Society
Website: www.rootsweb.ancestry.co.uk/~enghfhs/
Covers modern London borough of Hillingdon.

West London and Middlesex Family History Society
Website: www.lwmfhs.org.uk/
Covers London boroughs of Barnet, Brent, Camden, Ealing (northern part), Enfield, Haringey, Harrow, Islington, Westminster.

East Surrey Family History Society
Website: www.eastsurreyfhs.org.uk/
Covers London boroughs of Croydon, Kingston, Lambeth, Merton, Richmond, Southwark, Sutton and Wandsworth.

Woolwich and District Family History Society
Email: suhiwfhs@tiscali.co.uk
Website: www.woolwichfhs.org.uk/

Address: Sue Highley, 21 Crofton Avenue, Bexley, Kent, DA5 3AU
Covers Bexleyheath, Charlton, Eltham, Crayford, Greenwich, Plumstead, Welling, Woolwich.

North West Kent Family History Society
Email: secretary@nwkfhs.org.uk
Website: www.nwkfhs.org.uk
Covers London boroughs of Bexley, Bromley, Greenwich, Lewisham.

Select Bibliography

There are hundreds, if not thousands of books about family history. Some are general guides to the topic and cover many different topics. Some are more specific, and tackle one area of interest in depth. I have tried to include a fair sample of what is available now (I have excluded articles in magazines) and those which are particularly pertinent to London research, but please remember that more titles are appearing every year and information can quickly date. There is no need to buy or even read all of these books, but if your ancestor fits into one of the categories below, they may well be worth a look. Many libraries and record offices have a selection of some of these. TNA sells many of these in its shop.

D Annal, *Using Birth, Marriage and Death Records* (2000)
A Bevan, *Tracing your Ancestors in the National Archives* (2006)
S Bourne and A H Chicken, *Records of the Church of England: A Practical Guide* (1988)
G R Breed, *My Ancestors were Baptists* (1988)
P Chambers, *How to Find your Medieval Ancestors* (2005)
P Christian, *The Genealogists' Internet* (2005)
P Faithfull, *Basic Facts about Lunatics* (2002)
S Fowler, *Army Records for Family Historians* (2006)
S Fowler, *Using Poor Law Records* (2001)
M Gandy, *Tracing Catholic Ancestors* (2001)
M Gandy, *Tracing Nonconformist Ancestors* (2001)
J S W Gibson, *Quarter Sessions Records for Family Historians* (1995)
J Gibson and A Dell, *Tudor and Stuart Muster Rolls* (1991)
J S W Gibson and E Hampson, *Specialist Indexes for Family Historians* (2001)
J S W Gibson and C Rogers, *Poor Law Union Records,* vol. 1, *South East England and East Anglia* (1993)
J S W Gibson and C Rogers, *Poll Books, 1696–1872* (1994)
J S W Gibson and C Rogers, *Electoral Registers since 1832 and Burgers Rolls* (1990)
J S W Gibson and C Rogers, *Coroners' Records* (2000)
G Grannum, *Tracing your West Indian Ancestors* (2002)
K Grannum and N Taylor, *Wills and Other Probate Records: A Practical Guide* (2004)
D T Hawkings, *Criminal Ancestors: A Guide* (1996)
D Hey, *Journeys in Family History* (2004)
J Jurskowski, C Smith and D Crook, *Lay Taxes in England and Wales, 1188–1688* (1998)
P Kershaw and M Pearsall, *Immigrants and Aliens* (2000)

R Knights and G Yeo (eds), *Guide to Greater London History Sources*, vol. 1, *The City of London* (2000); vol. 2, *Middlesex* (2005)

W Leary, *My Ancestors were Methodists* (1999)

M E Mitchell, *Tracing Jamaican Ancestry* (1998)

E H Milligan and M J Thomas, *My Ancestors were Quakers* (1999)

R Paley, *Using Criminal Records* (2001)

S A Raymond, *Census, 1801–1911: A Guide for the Internet Era* (2009)

A Sherman, *My Ancestor was a Policeman* (2000)

W Spencer, *Army Service Records of the First World War* (2001)

W Spencer, *Records of the Militia and Volunteer Forces, 1757–1945* (1997)

W Spencer, *Medals: The Researchers' Companion* (2006)

R Swift, *Irish Immigrants in Britain, 1815–1914* (2002)

C Thomm, *Researching London Houses* (2005)

C Webb, *Greater London Cemeteries and Crematoria* (2005)

S Wade, *Tracing your Criminal Ancestors* (2009)

R Wenzerul, *Tracing your Jewish Ancestors? A Guide* (2008)

Finally, don't forget the monthly family history magazines available at most newsagents. These also include adverts of record agents who will, for a fee, undertake research on your behalf. Or you can contact the Association of Geneaologists and Record Agents at 29 Badger's Close, Horsham, West Sussex, RH12 5RU, and include a cheque for a list of the agents on their books. Their website is: www.agra.org.uk/

Books about London

There are thousands of these; ranging from general works to highly specialized ones. A few worth mentioning for a general coverage are as follows:

Victoria County History for Middlesex, vols 1–12, and for Essex, vols 1–10

The first two volumes concentrate general topics, such as prehistory, Domesday, religious buildings, education and so forth. Then each volume covers a number of parishes, covering numerous themes and are fully referenced. There are a few volumes for Hertfordshire, Kent and Surrey, but these are mostly county surveys, not detailed parish-by-parish accounts.

The VCHs are available online at www.british-history.ac.uk

The History Press have a large number of books in their 'Past' series which cover different parts of London, and their Images of London series (visual histories) covers many parts of the capital, too. The Godfrey maps are useful for the later nineteenth and early twentieth century, with their reproductions of Ordnance Survey maps, hundreds of which cover Greater London.

P Ackroyd, *London: A Biography* (2000)

C Hibbert and B Weinfield, *London Encyclopedia* (1983)

S Inwood, *A History of London* (1998)

D Lysons, *Environs of London*, 6 vols (1792–1800)

M Robbins, *Middlesex* (1953)

J Sharpe, *London and the Kingdom*, 3 vols (1894)

J Stow, *A Survey of London* (1598, many reprints)
J Thorne, *Handbook to the Environs of London*, 2 vols (1876)
E Walford, *Greater London*, 3 vols (1882)
J White, *London in the Twentieth Century* (2000)
J White, *London in the Nineteenth Century* (2007)

Websites

Perhaps the most useful single one is ancestry.co.uk. This is a subscription site, but can be viewed free at many public libraries and record offices. It includes many useful databases, the most important being those for the census 1841–1901, the indexes to births, marriages and deaths from 1837, the London/Middlesex parish registers (baptisms 1537–1906, marriages 1537–1921, burials 1537–1980). Most are searchable by name. There are also transcriptions of some London workhouse records, including creed registers, though these are not indexed by name.

The National Archives website. This hosts many important sources; including searchable databases of First World War soldiers' records, medal indexes, Prerogative Court of Canterbury Wills, 1389–1858, records of Royal Marines, ancient petitions, some immigration records and many more. Indexes are free, but a fee is payable to download the actual records (which can be seen free at the National Archives). It also hosts A2A, a searchable database of deposited archives in the UK.

The 1911 Census Index is available free on line at Findmypast, but again, a fee is payable to see the actual records (can be viewed free at TNA)

BT Archives website has telephone directories searchable by name.

Various newspapers can be viewed online, including the *Guardian*, *The Times* (from 1785) and the *Daily Mirror* (from 1903). All are subscription sites, but some public libraries offer *The Times* free. The British Library hosts a website covering forty-nine nineteenth-century newspapers, though none is specifically for London. Searching the indexes of these is free, but fees are payable for viewing the articles (unless viewed at institutions which subscribe to these, such as the British Library and TNA). All these can be searched by keyword, so are worth checking in case your ancestors' names appear.

Finally, www.nationalarchives.gov.uk/a2a/. This is a little used site by genealogists. It shouldn't be. It is a searchable database of UK archives which have been deposited in record offices, libraries and museums and which have been notified to the Historic Manuscripts Commission (now part of TNA). It lists collections, by name of organization; such as the name of a magistrates' court, a school, a church and so forth, and sometimes by individual. It will tell you where the collection is housed (assuming it exists) and might also list what the archive contains, with dates of each item in that archive, or at least covering dates. This helps locate material and so helps plan visits.

INDEX